Moonshot!

JOHN SCULLEY

FORMER CEO OF PEPSI AND APPLE, MENTOR, AND ENTREPRENEUR

Moonshot!

Game-Changing
Strategies to Build
Billion-Dollar Businesses

RosettaBooks
New York

FIRST EDITION 2014

18 17 16 15 14   1 2 3 4 5

Designed by Misha Beletsky
Cover design by Brad Mooberry

Cover and interior photography by Doug Menuez

Library of Congress Control Number: 2014946570
ISBN: 978-0-7953-4326-1

www.RosettaBooks.com

In memory of our parents,
Jack and Margaret Sculley,
who sacrificed so much for their three sons,
but tragically died too young
to see their sons become men.

And to my loving wife,
Diane Sculley.

CONTENTS

INTRODUCTION
AND HIGHLIGHTS

CUSTOMERS COME FIRST

Unless you have a deep understanding of the concept of exceptional customer experience, you may find your company out of business in a few years.

Why? Because the biggest Moonshot in years is happening right now: a dramatic, rapid shift from producers-in-control to customers-in-control.

This Moonshot is being propelled by a tsunami of exponentially expanding technologies never seen before: cloud computing, wireless sensors, Big Data, and mobile devices. This wave is causing economic power to shift, from business producers who worked hard to be in control of their customers, to increasingly smarter and smarter customers. This time the customers will be in control. As a lifelong business builder and consumer marketer, I am realizing how this Moonshot is so incredibly world-changing.

Those who fail to grasp what is happening will miss the future.

Those who learn to take advantage of serving a very smart customer will be the builders of future billion-dollar businesses.

Moonshot! is a book that will guide you through a journey, explaining, with solutions, how to do it.

Jeff Bezos says his customers are incredibly loyal; that is, until the moment someone else makes them a better offer. Customers are getting smarter. They don't even have to do much to get smarter. That's because we are in a new era of digital technology that will increasingly be about machine-learning systems and machine-to-machine communication, with no conscious human intervention required. The scale of customer data processing in the cloud will be so massive that the customer will have immediate information and individual power on an unprecedented level.

The Virgin brand has a reputation for exceptional customer experience so powerful that Richard Branson has been successful with it in all kinds of industries—from music, to mobile phone service, to airlines, and soon to consumer travel into space. One knows that a Virgin customer experience tolerates no compromises.

Elon Musk didn't just create an electric automobile. Tesla is an entirely new customer experience of how good personal transportation can be; it engages the customer in a complete end-to-end experience system.

Mayor Mike Bloomberg was already a legendary disruptive entrepreneur before he became New York City mayor for twelve years. He didn't have to bow to the lobbyists or special-interest groups. He treated New York City voters like customers. His efforts to collect data on so many aspects of New Yorkers' lives meant not only could the government operate more efficiently, but voters could find out what crimes or noise complaints have been reported in their neighborhood, how clean their local restaurants are, and even where the snowplows are after a blizzard.

MOONSHOTS

Moonshot is a term in Silicon Valley reserved for just a few of the most important innovations that reset everything following after them. The invention of the microprocessor was a Moonshot. So was the first useful personal computer, the Apple II; as was the first affordably priced desktop publishing system for creative people, the Mac. The creation of the World Wide Web was a Moonshot. So were the launches of Google Nexus One and Apple's iPhone. What each of these Moonshots has in common is they helped make ordinary, nontechnical, people smarter. They enabled what Steve Jobs used to call "tools for the mind."

The Moonshot I will unpack in this book is the leap computers have recently made from "productivity tools" to intelligent personal "assistants." A new generation of automated intelligent systems using machine learning and advanced data science has made this possible. IBM's Watson, Microsoft's Cortana, Google's Now and Apple's Siri are examples. This Moonshot is shifting economic power from traditional business producers to customers-in-control, and it's making customers incredibly smart. This Moonshot will change every industry of commerce in the world.

Propelling this Moonshot are four amazing digital technologies, each of which is growing at an exponential rate. Two of these technologies—cloud computing and mobile devices—are already touching billions of users. Soon, billions of miniature wireless sensors and a new generation of mathematical algorithms in data science incorporating artificially intelligent systems will analyze consumer behavior right down to the individual person, and automatically predict outcomes, helping people to make better informed decisions. Never has such powerful technology been commoditized so quickly, and become both so affordable and pervasive.

THE ADAPTIVE INNOVATOR

A new breed of entrepreneurs is emerging, putting customers first. They are raising the bar in customer-experience businesses with the incredibly ambitious goal of being ten times better than anything previously available. Thinking about your business plan as just an incremental improvement over the past will not be enough to succeed anymore. There has to be a better way, and I believe that somewhere in the world, some curious, optimistic, and very motivated people, in industry after industry, will figure out what that way is. The process starts with a few geniuses leading the way, then others become inspired. They are the entrepreneurs who attract others who will help them build transformative companies of the future.

I call this new breed of entrepreneurs the "adaptive innovators" and, as you will learn in this book, there has never been a better time to build a billion-dollar business. I will take you on a journey explaining why this opportunity is not only possible but probable, presenting the lessons I've learned from the best innovative minds, and offering many valuable insights and solutions that will help you become an adaptive innovator. I'm a hands-on builder who has been curious my whole life about the search for a better way to do things. I've had some big success and some big failures; being an adaptive innovator can be personally high risk but incredibly rewarding, too.

For adaptive innovators, as you will see, it's the customer plan, not the business plan that's important. What are the metrics of a customer plan? The rate of customer engagement and re-engagement; the conversion rate from consumer engagement to becoming a transacting customer; the scoring of customer satisfaction; the cost of customer acquisition; customer churn rate; the effectiveness of the cycle of customer management; the retention rate of a customer; and the lifetime value of a customer.

THE ADAPTIVE CORPORATION

One of the most important themes of this book is what I call "the adaptive corporation." Alvin Toffler wrote a groundbreaking book about *The Adaptive Corporation* in 1985. My goal here is to explain how the adaptive corporation in the present era requires a systemic design framework that is customer-driven, flexible to change, and inclusive of multiple-domain expertise. Traditional business processes will increasingly become obsolete, just as traditional business planning is much less useful than the customer plan in the adaptive corporation. I'll give examples of successful companies that became victims of their own success, explain why innovation happens at the edge of established industries, and explain why domain expertise in multiple domains is essential to taking advantage of much smarter customers, who also are far more powerful influencers in determining how quickly a business scales. And I must emphasize that the ability to scale supersedes the traditional profitability metrics we are accustomed to using in projecting a business's ability to survive and thrive.

You'll learn why traditional business and financial metrics of performance, while still helpful, are not as important as customer metrics are for adaptive innovators building a transformative business. And you'll discover that the traditional business process will become obsolete, and why transformative businesses are always about customer-centric data that updates itself in real time and usually with machine-to-machine communication.

Everything we thought we understood about running a successful business is open to better ways of doing things. It's an exciting time for optimists, entrepreneurs, and creative builders who want to learn how to build transformative businesses that take advantage of the growing power of customers.

THE ADAPTIVE MIDDLE CLASS

Here's a reality that adaptive innovators already know and that politicians choose to avoid: The incredibly successful middle-class aspirational lifestyle that has shaped economies in the West for the past sixty years is no longer sustainable in its present form. Meanwhile, emerging-market consumers numbering more than two billion are looking forward to joining the world's middle class by the early 2020s. I am very involved with building new businesses in Asia that are focused on the needs of their fast-growing middle class, and I'm impressed with the resourceful and frugal designs that adaptive innovators are creating to construct products and services at disruptive prices without compromising the customer experience. This time, we should expect that adaptive innovators from emerging markets will export creative solutions to the West that will appeal to our own middle class. Think of this as the era of the "adaptive middle class."

How will adaptive middle-class customers behave differently? They are making tradeoffs between ostentatious luxury and less-expensive alternatives. I used to buy several expensive Brioni suits at a time. Now I prefer Lululemon, Uniqlo, J. Crew, and Diesel jeans. Why? Because, as a customer, I love the feel of the fabric and, in the case of Uniqlo, the technology of the fabric, which breathes and adjusts automatically to the weather, whether it be hot or cold. I'm into comfort, but I also travel all the time, so I love that these moderately priced clothes pack so well in a carry-on bag. I don't often wear a watch anymore because it's more accurate and easier to tell time with my smartphone. I use subways and walk a lot in NYC because a ride in an NY taxi—when you can get one—is not a great customer experience. Since Uber arrived, I love the Uber customer experience.

THE ADAPTIVE MILLENNIAL

We have to pay special attention to what we can learn from the adaptive Millennial generation. They have never known a world without amazing technology. Their brains are hard-wired to rely on mobile devices and mobile apps for almost everything. They don't watch much traditional television. They don't read newspapers or books all the way through. They skim for information. They are on overload with social media. When they write, their preference is to abbreviate. They are the best educated and most underemployed generation in history. They are, by necessity, becoming start-up entrepreneurs because traditional jobs are hard to find. Their aspirations include and often stress the social value of their work.

The adaptive Millennials haven't become addicted to conspicuous consumption. They job hop, when they can get jobs. Sharing things works for them. They prefer to rent rather than own, as it takes less capital. They will conserve their spending by economizing where they eat, but will still splurge for a ticket to a hip-hop music event. And they save more than older generations. The adaptive Millennial generation will be early adopters of many transformative businesses.

HOW THIS BOOK CAN HELP YOU SUCCEED

The real focus of my book is on solutions—how transformative businesses can actually be built. This starts, of course, with creating a compelling business idea, the "billion-dollar concept." I will draw on real-world examples from rapidly growing companies that I am either well aware of or personally involved with today to lay out groundbreaking strategies that successful adaptive innovators are employing to create huge new companies. **One of the most important of these, for example, is to deliver an incredible customer experience on a quality level never before experienced.**

The most powerful model for future success, I believe, is to combine an exceptional customer experience with a disruptive price. We will also lay out specific, game-changing tools for success that resourceful adaptive innovators can access to increase the chances of building truly transformative new businesses.

I believe we are entering an unprecedented era for major new business opportunities. While I have always been an optimist, I think this is the most exciting time of my life to be in business. I hope my message inspires innovators inside and outside of existing companies to create a new generation of billion-dollar businesses.

—John Sculley
September 2014

PART I

Moonshot!

1.

MOONSHOT!

I actually think every individual is now an entrepreneur, whether they recognize it or not.
        —Reid Hoffman,
            cofounder and executive
            chairman of LinkedIn

In November 1982, few people outside of the Bay Area had ever heard of Silicon Valley, so I was very curious about what my day ahead would be like. At the time, as president of Pepsi-Cola Company, I had been invited to Apple, which then had just $500 million in revenues and was looking for a CEO. As I drove from my hotel, Rickey's Hyatt House in Palo Alto, to Cupertino, I looked around expecting to see some glass-walled, modern buildings peppering the landscape similar to the ones I had become accustomed to seeing on Route 128 surrounding Boston. But this was Silicon Valley, and I was soon to discover that this foreign (to me) world beat to a very different drum. Driving up to Bandley Drive in Cupertino, I thought I must be at the wrong address for Apple Computers' headquarters: It was just five small, one- and two-floor, tilt-up-wall-construction buildings tucked into a residential area.

This was the first time that I met Steve Jobs. After an hour with the then Apple CEO, Mike Markkula, Steve joined us, and shortly afterward he and I split off. Steve and I spent the next hour sizing each other up. I was immediately struck by how self-confident and articulate he was, with his sweeping description of how personal computers were going to be the most important educational tool ever in mankind's history. In those days Steve—at twenty-seven—was healthy, strikingly handsome with thick black hair and dark, penetrating eyes. I had arrived in my business casual khaki pants, open-collar blue shirt, and blue blazer. I immediately felt out of place as Steve, along with everyone else I was to meet, wore blue jeans and T-shirts.

Steve took me across Bandley Drive to a one-story building called Bandley II. I couldn't help but notice a black-and-white Jolly Roger pirate flag flapping from a flagpole atop the building. Once inside, I followed Steve to a small lab with an engineer's bench jammed with lots of test equipment. My eyes quickly focused on a bright ten-inch display and, next to it, a slight, young engineer with a beaming smile named Andy Hertzfeld.

Steve suddenly got very serious. "Nobody outside Apple has ever before seen what you are about to see," he said with gravity. "We are creating the world's first personal media computer that is designed to be incredibly easy for nontechnical people to use and it will be affordably priced. This prototype will become the Mac . . . and it's going to change the world."

On a nearby keyboard, Andy started typing quickly, and suddenly five animated little Pepsi cans danced across the screen. "This is just the beginning of a revolution where people will be able to publish their own content, combining beautiful fonts, graphics, and even animations like this. It's going to be insanely great!" Steve added with a flourish.

When Gutenberg invented the printing press in Mainz, Rhineland, in 1436, it later enabled Aldus in Venice to print books and sell them from town to town. Nothing like that had ever been possible before, and its effect was to open the minds of anyone who could read to provocative ideas. History, science, poetry, and theology suddenly spread across Europe. This Renaissance was the cultural awakening from the Dark Ages and a thousand years of feudal society to a new world-changing era for mankind.

Steve Jobs had created a cover story for my visit in order to explain to the young Mac development team why I was there and why he was showing me, an outsider, Apple's most secret project. Steve had told them that I was the CEO of Pepsi-Cola Company and that I was potentially the first big corporate customer for the Mac. "So, we should impress him . . . ," he directed. At the time, I didn't fully appreciate how technically advanced and challenging it had been just to make those black-and-white Pepsi cans dance on that small ten-inch display.

This moment was my introduction to the creation of a Moonshot. I had first heard the term in 1961 when then President John F. Kennedy uplifted a still-in-shock American public from the Soviet's successful 1957 launch of Sputnik, the first satellite, into space. JFK had eloquently proclaimed that, before that decade was over, we would send a man to the moon and safely bring him back. It was inspiring . . . it was maybe possible . . . but it would be incredibly hard.

Years later, on July 20, 1969, I remember standing on the Sheep Meadow in Manhattan's Central Park with 20,000 other people, watching man's first landing on the moon on a huge screen. The crowd was hushed as the lunar vehicle module, the Eagle, made numerous attempts to land. When it finally came to rest and the hatch opened, astronauts Neil Armstrong and Buzz Aldrin descended the ladder. At exactly 4:18 p.m. Eastern time, Neil Armstrong became the first man ever to step onto the surface of the moon, uttering those famous words: "One small step for man, one giant leap for mankind." At this moment, a deafening cheer erupted and everyone in the crowd hugged one another in celebration. This was the granddaddy of all Moonshots, and it was amazing.

The first man to step onto the moon in 1969 never would have been able to make that journey if the U.S. had not paved the way with a "tubes-to-transistor" moment. The telemetry required to navigate the Apollo 11 rocket ship to the moon would never have fit into the spacecraft if lightweight, miniaturized transistors had not been commercially developed and adapted for this purpose. NASA underwrote this critical tubes-to-transistors research, which led to the founding of Intel by Gordon Moore and Bob Noyce, among other significant high-technology firms. I realized only years later that Neil Armstrong's success inspired many students to take up science, math, and engineering because it was now cool. And some of these students later used their technical skills and creativity to launch the personal computer era—a breakthrough I witnessed firsthand with Steve Jobs.

Larry Page is a business leader who is changing the world by using his exceptional talent and Google's success to continue to make creative leaps. Moonshot is now part of the Silicon Valley lexicon, a designation reserved for only the most game-changing disruptive innovations. Steven Levy's book *In the Plex* talks admiringly about Google and Larry Page's "healthy disrespect for the impossible." Larry Page is indeed leading the way today with amazing Moonshots like driverless cars. No one has been more inspiring about the possibilities of Moonshots than Google with their creation of an annual Silicon Valley event dubbed "Solve for ×." Astro Teller, Google's captain of Moonshots, calls this, "10× thinking that doesn't break the laws of physics about clearly defined problems."[1] He goes on to say that 10× thinking with a low probability of success is a more inspiring and passionate goal than making the bottom line ten percent better with a high probability of success. One of the most talented individuals who worked with me at Apple is Megan Smith, VP of Google Labs' Solve for ×, further illustrating that Google is committing their best people to 10× innovation. Big corporations aren't usually wired to think this way. Google is.

THE PERSONAL COMPUTER MOONSHOT:
WOZ, THE GENIUS INVENTOR

Steve Wozniak invented the first really useful personal computer. He is a rare breed, a "disruptive innovator" genius like Thomas Edison. "So, Woz what did you want to be?" I recently asked him when we were sitting around and chatting. "Well, I never really cared about starting a company," he answered, "that was all Steve Jobs' idea. We actually started five companies, but the one that survived was Apple. Before Apple, I was perfectly happy working at Hewlett-Packard and being an engineer, but I wanted to be the best engineer in the entire world. So I had to figure out how to design things with pen and paper and I would design minicomputers because I didn't have any money. But then HP had this wonderful program, where engineers, if they were working on something that interested them, would let them take parts home for free." He said: "I used to do that and build things. So I would build things with one-dollar chips using some hacker approaches that were being built by other people for thousands of dollars. Why? Because I was a natural hacker and I wanted things for myself and I really wanted to build a computer."

What drove Woz to invent the personal computer? I think it was the passion that emerged when this shy but gifted eleven-year-old realized that he was just naturally brilliant at mathematics. He can still solve any kind of math problem in his head. Woz realized that so much of computing is about math: when to load registers, what you load into each register, when you execute commands, all those kinds of things.

Woz would go to the library and look up technical papers on signal processing of various minicomputers being sold back in the early 1970s. From this research, he just kept increasing his domain expertise about computers. In short order, he learned an incredible amount about computers as they existed at that time.

At the same time, he was a hacker, and so he figured out

7

novel ways of hacking, solving problems cheaply that others solved expensively. So that was a different domain. He coupled the hacker's domain with the traditional computer science domain. All self-taught.

When it came to designing the Apple I board, he solved a problem that hadn't been solved before, in a very inexpensive hacker's way. Woz's first computer, the Apple I, was for hobbyists. The second computer he developed, the Apple II, was for the rest of us. Steve Jobs had declared an incredible vision: "Hey, why don't we build a computer that isn't just a kit with a circuit board connected to a TV, but a complete, easy-to-use, all-in-one device?" And guided by Steve's vision, Woz built the Apple II.

Woz recently told me one of my now favorite stories about him. Back in the late '70s, he'd never been to Las Vegas but had always wanted to go there. Apple was taking the Apple II to the Las Vegas CES, Consumer Electronics Show, for the first time. Because Apple had almost no money, only three people were going to make the trip: Mike Markkula, who was cofounder and head of marketing; Apple's CEO at the time, Mike Scott; and Steve Jobs. But Woz wanted to go and made a proposition to the three: "If I can design a floppy disk drive, would I be allowed to go on the trip to Las Vegas with you?" This was like less than a month away. They said, "Yes," because there was no such thing as a floppy disk drive in the market at that time.

Woz told me that he stayed up night after night with no sleep. He worked around the clock for over a week, churning calculations in his head, figuring out ways to hack it and build it. He did get to go to Las Vegas for the first time, and he brought the first floppy disk drive for the Apple II computer. No one in the world had ever seen a floppy disk drive for a personal computer before. There were disk drives for big minis and mainframe computers, but these things cost thousands of dollars. The idea that you could have an affordable floppy disk for a personal computer didn't seem possible then. Up until this point, an Apple II used a tiny tape recorder to archive its programming code. Inspired by the lure of a first trip to Vegas, Woz invented the first floppy disk drive.

Back in the 1970s, other highly talented disruptive innovators like Bill Gates, Steve Jobs, and Larry Ellison also dropped out of college, as Woz had done, to become entrepreneurs. Why? Computer science programs just weren't teaching the new technologies needed to reinvent the computer industry around the microprocessor and the new kinds of software it required.

Many times, my wife, Diane, and I have watched Woz create seemingly impossible math puzzles and then somehow do massive calculations in his head, no paper required, to solve the puzzle. Truly magical moments, and I have no idea how he does it. But his knack paid off big-time. Woz first created the Apple I, a circuit board with chips and DRAM memory. He and Steve Jobs sold it through Paul Terrell's first Byte Shop for $666.66. Later, Woz invented the Apple II, which included a never-before-seen way to display fonts and graphics on a color TV monitor, a feat no one previously thought was possible.

THE DERIVATIVE EFFECTS OF WOZ'S INVENTION

It was Steve Jobs who saw the promise in Woz's computer inventions and came up with the idea to create the Apple II, an all-in-one-box solution that was easy to learn how to use. One didn't have to program the Apple II as you did with the earlier hobbyist computers, you just inserted a software application into it, and it did useful things like create a spreadsheet, write a letter, or store some data you could retrieve later. Steve Jobs designed the Apple II to have a beautiful ABS plastic case with a built-in keyboard. So began the first computer industry Moonshot of a truly personal computer that was affordable for the average person. Steve Jobs was a different kind of genius from Woz. Steve was not an engineer, but a visionary with a noble cause and an instinctive designer's talent for envisioning end-to-end systems. Steve Jobs was a systemic designer who could not only zoom out and connect the dots, but could zoom in and simplify computers in a way that made them both incredibly easy to use and consistently beautiful machines.

Steve Jobs had a genius ability to see the future possibility of other genius inventions and how to turn these inventions into products that would actually change the world. Steve Jobs likened computers to "bicycles for the mind." Give people computer tools, he believed, and let them change the world one person at a time. He saw that his machines had to be really easy to use and inexpensive enough that most people could buy one. Steve sweated every detail. He had the charisma and focused determination to drive the success of first the Apple II and then the Mac.

Bill Gates is also a true genius. He is very technical and is a self-taught computer scientist who is quite different from Steve Jobs and Woz. Bill Gates is an adaptive innovator who saw that the future of personal computing was going to be about software licensing and creating software applications that could be sold on a disk in a box on a retail store shelf. He had the most amazing focus. The combination of these qualities made him the best business competitor I ever knew. Everyone in the industry was gunning for Bill, but he never lost his focus or his optimism. He was relentless in building Microsoft into the overwhelmingly dominant force in software.

Steve Jobs, in the early days when I arrived, was the visionary, but he was inflexible and trusted only his own instincts. He had to make every important decision in the Mac group. So in those days, Steve Jobs was not yet an adaptive innovator like Bill Gates, because Steve Jobs was not pragmatic, as Bill Gates was. Even after he left Apple in 1985 and founded NeXT and acquired a small media animation technology company, PIXAR, from George Lucas, Steve was still unwilling to compromise on anything. NeXT and PIXAR both almost went bankrupt. Despite this, Steve's genius as a "systemic designer" was important to both of these companies' eventually becoming extremely important to the future of Silicon Valley. While NeXT failed as a computer company, Steve Jobs later sold it to Apple for $400 million in 1996, and the NeXT operating system became the Mac operating system (OS). By the mid-1990s, the ever-improving computational performance predicted by Moore's Law made it possible to make computer-generated animated movies, and PIXAR switched from being a computer company into a creative animated film company—later sold to Disney for more than $7 billion.

By the time Steve Jobs returned to Apple, twelve years after leaving in 1985, he had matured as an executive. He was still Steve Jobs the brilliant systemic designer, but he was now also an adaptive innovator. He adapted the then failing Mac into the successful iMac as the easy-to-use portal device for the recently introduced World Wide Web, using the Netscape browser invented by Jim Clark and Marc Andreessen. It was the perfect adaptive-innovator product at exactly the right time, and it also was the perfect systemic designer product. The gumdrop design of the iMac at that time and its bright attractive colors became the wake-up call for high technology that the consumer electronics digital era had begun. The world loved the concept and the iMac design. By then, Steve Jobs' first decision on returning to Apple as CEO was to cancel the disastrous policy of licensing the Mac OS; a decision made after I had left Apple and a policy that almost bankrupted the company. Later, Steve followed up with another product, the iPod, which combined both his end-to-end systems genius and his love for technology and music. The iPod also demonstrated that Steve Jobs had evolved into an adaptive innovator. By 1997, Steve had expanded his domain expertise to include a new domain for him of consumer entertainment. While it seems obvious today that high tech and entertainment are domains that have converged, it wasn't obvious before Steve had his success in the mid-1990s with both PIXAR's animated movies and the iMac, iPod, and iTunes. His multiple-domain expertise combined computing with recorded music in the beautiful, easy-to-use device and end-to-end system of iPod to iTunes. He redefined the recording industry with the iTunes store, which allowed consumers to buy songs individually for ninety-nine cents, rather than buy the entire album. And Silicon Valley was amazed that Steve made the iPod fully compatible with Windows computers—something the Steve Jobs I knew in the 1980s never would have done.

Unquestionably, the iPhone was Steve Jobs' greatest Moonshot ever. It is the perfect example of brilliant adaptive innovation. It again converged expertise in multiple domains: Low-cost, miniaturized consumer electronic components, able to run a long time on a single battery charge, converged with mobile wireless technology. Timing is everything in the high-tech world, and it would have been impossible for the iPhone to do what it does so well until wireless providers like AT&T made the shift from a slower 2G to enhanced-speed 3G, with expanded services like GPS and faster photo and video transfers. The total end-to-end solution was presented in Steve's handsome systems design of the smartphone, coupled with his brilliant concept of the App Store. The iPhone was a masterpiece, and, through it, the smartphone became the world's most indispensable cultural instrument. Google engineer Andy Rubin was an incredibly smart "fast follower" of the iPhone, with the creation of the open source and free Android platform, while Microsoft found itself completely left out! We will talk later in the book about how mobile devices are changing the world. And the revolution all started with Steve Jobs' iPhone!

THE TSUNAMI OF TECHNOLOGY

Today there is a tsunami that involves four exponential technologies converging at such speeds that they are ushering in a second digital age. Peter Diamandis, in his book *Abundance*, was the first to explain that, in this new digital era, there is no scarcity of resources. In fact, he points out the most important digital technologies are actually growing exponentially.

The first leg of this technology tsunami is cloud computing. Operational only in the last five or six years, it is an idea we already take for granted today. Why exponential? The power of processing has grown exponentially. If we go back to 2008, some estimates were that there were 800 exabytes of data in the world. (An exabyte is 10 to the 18th power.) Here's a simple story I heard that gives you a sense of just how large an exabyte of data is: Imagine you had just a single DVD and you filled it up with as much information as it could possibly hold. Then imagine a 747's passenger cabin filled with DVDs each packed with data. It would take over 15,000 747s filled with such DVDs to just hold a single exabyte of data. By 2020, estimates are there will be 40,000 exabytes of data! Of course, these are really only guesstimates. In parallel, the cost of data storage in the cloud has dropped in the past two years, from about $5 a gigabyte to less than twenty-five cents a gigabyte. HP CEO Meg Whitman recently announced that her company has invented a way to shrink a large cloud data center down into a refrigerator-size box that HP calls "The Machine." IBM announced it would invest $3 billion on R&D for new microprocessor materials like graphene that may further improve data processing performance by orders of magnitude. We are still in the early days of exponential performance possibilities.

The cloud is far more significant than just a big and more affordable back-office computer system. It enables us to do things we couldn't do before. It fundamentally revalues data. Think about this analogy: In the nineteenth-century Industrial Age, flowing rivers were harnessed to power factories. In the twentieth century, the same flowing river water began to power electricity-generating turbines that are distributed by cables anywhere. Electricity is an indispensable resource and we just assume we can always plug into it. Sometime in the future, cloud data processing and storage will become a utility like city water, electricity, or natural gas that one just plugs into as a customer service.

The second leg of this technology tsunami is termed the Internet of Things, which Cisco's CEO, John Chambers, has forecasted will include 40 billion wireless connected devices by the early 2020s. How is this possible when there are only 7 billion people on the planet and there are only 6 billion mobile cellphones? The answer is, we are in a new era of miniaturized sensors that can communicate wirelessly. Not to humans, but machine-to-machine. This will change every industry and will help make customers smarter. For example, imagine a GE jet engine with 500 onboard sensors monitoring and generating wireless data in flight over an ocean, sending automatic reports back to the airline and to maintenance organizations en route, and to GE too. Or a consumer example might be Apple's new health kit, which creates a new wellness vertical domain platform on top of its operating system, which will enable app developers to use data captured from the ten onboard sensors built into the iPhone. And wireless sensors will be used to monitor medical metrics for patients at home in real time.

When I arrived in Silicon Valley over thirty years ago, it was the early days of the microprocessor. Now the age of sensors is just dawning. Sensors are able to sense light, sound, and heat, and measure bodily motion . . . all kinds of things. Increasingly, data transfer is the machine-to-machine relay of information. Most of these billions of wirelessly connected sensors will invisibly connect machine-to-machine with data stored in the cloud, where the information will be processed in real time with astonishing speed.

Note the chain sequence of Moonshots in recent years: The Moonshot invention of the microprocessor led to the Moonshot creation of the Internet, which led to the World Wide Web, which led to the Moonshot of Google. In each subsequent reality, people became smarter. Now we are in the era of the Internet of Things, where billions of miniature sensors will use machine-learning systems. This time, it's not just people getting smarter, but machines that are getting smarter, too. Ray Kurzweil, now head of Google's engineering lab, has long predicted what he describes as The Singularity, an event some expect to happen around 2040 or 2045, when machines will achieve consciousness and become a new inanimate species that will be smarter than humans. Whether you choose to believe this prediction or not, machine learning that doesn't require human intervention is already happening, and its growth is exponential.

The third leg of this technological tsunami effect is Big Data: aggregations of large data sets, often from multiple sources and made up of structured or unstructured data. That unstructured data might be a consumer's GPS location using satellites, tracking exactly where that consumer is via transmissions from a mobile device. Or, the unstructured data might be social media. It might be video. It might be audio. It might be text. And, the consumer data might include both structured as well as unstructured data—all kinds of different data sources. This data will allow companies to predict what people will want and why they want it.

When I was in Silicon Valley, we were all using calculus and differential equation math to empower knowledge workers with structured data tools like relational databases. The way engineers work with unstructured data today is very different. It's all about making predictions from seemingly unrelated data sources using probability mathematics. As a graduate student, and later as a consumer market researcher, I became very familiar with Bayesian statistics, Markov chain analysis, and Monte Carlo game theory. Novelties only decades ago, these are the very practical tools today. This field of mathematics is popularly known as data science, and it's centered on predictive analytics. It's termed "predictive" because we are only determining the *probability* of data accuracy combining all kinds of unrelated data sources. Previously, data modeling created simulations of hypothetical events by manipulating the numeric values of just a very small number of variables; then calculating the results. Probability math gives us the ability to simultaneously consider hundreds, even thousands of attributes with new data being updated in real time from hundreds, even thousands, of sensors. Even a decade ago, it would have been impossible to compute so many concurrent calculations in real time. With the efficiency of cloud computing, these operations are now both practical and quite affordable.

There are many examples of very smart people missing the significance of this emerging disruptive technology tool. A piece of recent history underscores this point: Using data science, experts can gain the insights needed to decide on behavior and influence it. In President Obama's 2012 presidential campaign, as reported in the *M.I.T. Technology Review*, his campaign managers had a tool that Governor Romney's team didn't. Obama's forces had begun using data science in his first presidential campaign in 2008, and they had accumulated a lot of baseline information about his voters. His 2012 team updated the databases. For Obama to be re-elected, he had to overcome a disastrous change in sentiment marked by the 2010 midterm elections. "Two years after Barack Obama's election as president," the *Review* reported, "Democrats suffered their worst defeat in decades. The congressional majorities that had given Obama his legislative successes, reforming the health insurance and financial markets, were swept away in the midterm elections..."

Months before the election, while measuring the president's popularity with his base, Obama's team discovered an important fact: The president's most loyal supporters were not as enthusiastic about him in 2012 as they were in 2008. But they also discovered that Mitt Romney's conservative base wasn't very enthusiastic about him, either. Experienced marketers know how difficult it is to significantly change a consumer's behavior. The Obama team didn't need to significantly change the minds of Obama supporters; they needed only to nudge them enough so they would show up at the polls.

Many advisers on the Romney team were highly educated and experienced business consultants who had a lot of structured data experience. The Romney team conducted traditional surveys, typically weekly, where they tracked a small set of key indicators with important demographic groups in swing voter states. "But Romney's data science team was less than one-tenth the size of Obama's analytics department," the *Review* reported. Meanwhile, the Obama data scientists were tracking hundreds of attributes, using unstructured data from all kinds of sources including social media tracking and TV viewing habits, all the time. As part of their nudge campaign, the Obama advisers concluded that political advertisers had been asking the wrong questions. This led the Obama team "to reimagine the targeting process" and to reach those targets more effectively. For example, they weren't content with knowing viewer habits of a particular niche. They had actually narrowed the message targets down to hundreds of facts about each potential voter, with detailed information resulting from massive data processing that used sophisticated predictive algorithms. They studied every way each individual watched television and used social media. Many of Obama's 2008 Hispanic voters, it turned out, enjoyed watching Spanish language soaps and shopping network shows in the middle of the night.

Then, using this data-backed knowledge, they were able to accurately know whom they most needed to target and when and where to reach them with the right messages. As a result of such remarkably precise tactics, President Obama was re-elected with fifty-one percent of the popular vote, despite the enormous midterm setbacks of 2010.

By the time of the election, the Obama team had consistently outmaneuvered the very smart Romney experts simply because the Obama team had a tool that they knew how to use; the opposition didn't have it or even fully understand its application.

Now imagine a story like this being repeated over and over in industry after industry with the crucial differentiator being: Those who master data science and those who don't. This is the landscape of business change unfolding today.

Combine the power of cloud computing with wireless sensors, allowing you to capture all kinds of data, and the use of unstructured data through predictive analytics, and you have a technological tsunami of epic magnitude. We are in a perfect storm in data science. It is built on the huge systemic changes, which match in importance the original commercialization of the Internet that took place decades earlier.

The fourth leg of the exponential technology tsunami is all about mobile. The smartphone has become the consumer's most important cultural instrument.

In January 1993, I gave one of the keynotes at the Consumer Electronics Show in Las Vegas, where I outlined Apple's breakthrough insight at the time marking the convergence of computing, content, and communications. This convergence foreshadowed a new era we predicted for Personal Digital Assistants (PDAs): small handheld devices with no keyboards and powered with artificial intelligence. Doug Solomon, then Apple's head of corporate strategy, foresaw this convergence at a gathering we'd organized six months earlier. We'd invited leaders from the entertainment and technology industries to Hakone, Japan, to hear and discuss Doug's analysis. In those days, it was rare for the leaders of these different sectors to get together at all. At Hakone, thanks to Apple's talented special-event producer, Satjiv Cahill, we created the perfect venue for these senior executives from major international corporations and different domains—leaders who'd never met one another before—to discuss technologies that would change their industries.

In early 1993, the concept of the PDA probably sounded a little weird to the CES audience, since it was years before digital mobile "feature phones." At the time I didn't realize the controversy I would be creating when I predicted that the PDA industry would eventually see a billion of these mobile devices in the world. The press that followed my speech was scorching, attacking me for making such a ridiculous assertion. After all, the criticism contended, if one added up all the PCs cumulatively ever sold by 1993, it still measured only a few hundred million units! One highly respected newspaper accused me of predicting that Apple was going to sell over a billion of its expected Newton PDA. This paper was so well regarded that others used its story as fact, never bothering to check out that I actually wasn't forecasting Newton's sales. The lesson here: If you seek out publicity, you can't complain just because someone publishes your story in a wrong and unflattering way. The higher one gets, the further the media likes to see them fall. If this bothers you, just learn to get over it. Life isn't just about good publicity.

Smartphones are no longer just about being phones. More importantly, they actually *are* our personal digital assistants. Our smartphones already are indispensable. Consumer apps are indispensable too. Personalized digital assistants, like Apple's Siri, have been a novelty until now. But all kinds of improved assistants, including Siri, will get better soon. We aren't far off from when personalized digital assistants will know nearly everything about us and a lot more about everything we want or need.

While the first Siri was a novelty, we are already in a second generation of smarter, nonhuman virtual assistants like Google Now, Microsoft's Cortana, and a very smart virtual assistant optimized for Spanish speakers called Sherpa, created by my friend Xabier Uribe-Etxebarria in Bilbao, Spain. Sherpa goes a step further than other PDAs, as it archives a history of each user, enabling it to get smarter as a result; Sherpa connects this personalized data directly to a user's e-commerce transactions.

These early virtual assistants enable users to ask questions and get meaningful answers instantly. More and more, the future will be about machine systems virtually learning from millions of sensors. Inevitably, normal people just using their mobile devices will become smarter consumers. For example, customers using their mobile smartphone will automatically know if a particular retailer has the best products, at the cheapest prices, when they are walking past a store in a mall. The ability today to be able to input how customers feel about a product, or refer a product or service to others from their mobile devices, will become easier, and all this information automatically will be fed into a multitude of cloud systems. Using machine-to-machine (M2M) learning and end-to-end information systems that will be ten times or a hundred times or a thousand times better than we have today, these M2M learning systems, using millions of sensors for data inputs, will know an incredible amount about you. I'll leave the many scenarios to your imagination, but they are almost endless. Machine-to-machine computation and machine learning will automatically make consumers smarter customers, for one very important reason: Machines don't get tired like humans do.

As that happens, economic power will pivot from producers-in-control to customer-in-control. Those producers like Amazon, eBay, Apple, Google, Baidu, Alibaba, and Tencent—which create end-to-end consumer-empowering systems—will be the big winners. What's different in this second digital age? The game-changing future in computer science won't be just about better knowledge worker tools, it will be about artificially intelligent, very smart, very personalized systems using unstructured data and predictive analytics. Incredibly powerful . . . customizable to every individual on the planet . . . disruptively affordable . . . and *capable of changing every industry in the global economy!*

TODAY'S BIG MOONSHOT: CUSTOMERS-IN-CONTROL

The economic derivative effect of the combination of these four exponential growth digital technologies is creating what I believe is one of the biggest

Moonshot effects of all. That is the permanent, ir-reversible power shift from producers-in-control to customers-in-control.

These incredible technologies are evolving at an unbelievable speed. They are now affordable to both corporations and to individual entrepreneurs. They have the power to reduce the overhead costs of an organization by using automated processes to replace many "white-collar" middle managers. I think about it this way: Outsourcing and heavy lifting robots have replaced many of the traditional medium-skilled jobs in manufacturing. Now very smart, end-to-end computer systems, along with very smart robots, will cause many white-collar jobs to be eliminated. Middle managers have traditionally managed the workers who are in charge of important work processes, and middle managers are measured on improving performance by the quality of their management decisions like hiring talented workers, training workers to do their job better, resolving disputes when they arise, responding to customer issues, meeting important dates, and handing work off to other middle managers. But what if companies had innovative better ways that were disruptively cheaper, faster, and more convenient to solve these issues and that it became obvious that an investment in capital was clearly better than an investment in labor? In a scenario where it might take fewer workers, it might also take fewer middle managers, as computers are better than humans at some things, but obviously not everything. It's not just about the heavy lifting jobs that are at risk; it's now about the smart management jobs that are exposed to disruption too.

Consumers now have access to real-time information on products and services, with complete price transparency and with product reviews from a wide range of web services, notably Amazon. They also have constant contact with their friends, who are instantly connected with various social media sites like Facebook. And they can mobilize huge groups of supporters in no time, almost anywhere in the world. This is perhaps the biggest Moonshot of all time. It is happening now and is rapidly transferring power from producers to consumers.

The power shift to the customer-in-control will open up unprecedented opportunities for entrepreneurs. It will also cause disruptions to traditional industries like never before.

A traditional way of managing might have been to ask: "How can we do this function cheaper?" Now that it is practical and affordable to make customers much smarter, we have no choice but to make producer businesses smarter than they have ever been to keep up with their more empowered customers. So business systems have to be conceptualized and adapted in innovative ways.

Those companies that don't adapt by refocusing their business models and organizations squarely on the consumer will not survive, in my view. Those willing to adapt have the opportunity to both survive and prosper.

THE NETWORK EFFECT

My good friend Bob Metcalfe is co-inventor of Ethernet and the originator of Metcalfe's Law, which quantifies the value of a network. Bob observed that the Internet was enabling computers to connect to computers, which would then connect to other computers. He is also a mathematician and realized that this network effect can be roughly approximated by saying that the value of a computer network system is equal to the square root of the number of other computers that are connected to your computer. Today, Metcalfe's Law, more commonly referred to as the network effect, is as important as Moore's Law. It is a vivid demonstration of exponential growth and supplements the points already made about today's game-changing technologies. The network effect explains why companies like Facebook, Twitter, and LinkedIn have grown so quickly and multiplied their numbers of users to very massive levels so quickly. It's why Facebook, watching Snapchat draw away their younger Facebook users, was willing to acquire Instagram for $1 billion. The network effect explains how Facebook was able to surge from no mobile revenue to a level of fifty percent of its revenues coming from mobile in just two and a half years. Similarly, the network effect explains why it made sense for Facebook to pay $19 billion (mostly with Facebook stock) for WhatsApp in order to get to its 450 million mobile messaging users.

The network effect changes everything, because now consumers are the key influencers for every service on the web. Consumers rate products and services for other consumers; consumers also make recommendations through their networks. Knowing a consumer's behavior profile will increase the value of an instant special discount a producer wants to offer a consumer who is standing right in front of a shelf display in a retail store. **The source of influence also changes the entire dynamics of marketing. The power of customer ratings, customer recommendations, and customer complaints cannot be overstated.**

Enormous opportunities exist for a new breed of entrepreneurs, whom I call "adaptive innovators," as well as for enlightened companies, "adaptive corporations," that embrace this new age of exponential technologies and the new world of the customer-in-control.

ADAPTIVE INNOVATORS: TODAY'S BUSINESS BUILDERS

Thus far, I have mentioned true geniuses who have created world-changing Moonshots during my lifetime. Most were disruptive inventors like Woz, Gordon Moore, Bob Noyce, and Andy Grove. Steve Jobs was a systemic designer genius who later evolved to become a genius adaptive innovator. Paraphrasing Bill Gates in a recent Charlie Rose interview, it's amazing how much Steve Jobs achieved in his life with his genius for intuitive design sense, as he really wasn't that technical. Two other examples today of systemic designer geniuses include Jeff Bezos, who in Amazon has created an utterly unique e-commerce system that is disrupting retailing, and Elon Musk, who will likely disrupt the auto industry with his Tesla electric car. Bezos and Musk are also adaptive innovators, and it's the adaptive innovators who really excite me today.

Adaptive innovators, I believe, are today's best entrepreneurs. They are highly motivated, highly curious individuals set on their own personal missions, which I call their "noble causes." They do not have to be geniuses like Steve Jobs and Bill Gates. Rather, today they can harness these exponential technologies at affordable prices. **Combining their own domain expertise in multiple business sectors with advanced technologies, adaptive innovators will create transformative businesses on a scale never seen before.**

What have I done in my life that I've really been proud of and truly enjoyed? Writing this book has allowed me to reflect thoughtfully about that question. The world runs on different types of skills and talents and they all have importance. I'm clearly not comparable to Steve Jobs. He was a systemic designer with exceptional instinctive talents. He was passionately motivated and willing to sacrifice a lot of other things in order to accomplish the many things he achieved in his life.

The best description of what I have done in my life is not as a CEO but as a builder, an adaptive innovator. My life has been focused on transformative businesses. I have focused on developing expertise in businesses that are at moments of transformation. I am curious by nature, and my business experience has enabled a personal journey that has crossed many industries.

Since I left Apple, and largely based on my experience working with the Newton (the first commercial, handheld computer using artificial intelligence) and on The Knowledge Navigator (the concept video of the sort available today on YouTube) while at Apple, I delved deeply into mobile software and mobile services, certain this would be a fascinating part of our future. I became very interested in financial services because my brother Arthur was doing breakthrough work in this domain when he cofounded Intralinks, the first software-as-a-service company for business-to-business. It's now a public company on the New York Stock Exchange. And I've been involved in many other financial service businesses, including an overseas company I recently helped cofound, a credit finance and supply-chain acquisition corporation called Inflexionpoint. I'm passionate about the general world of the supply chain—because it's an absolutely key underpinning to everything that we do in a global economy.

I'm also now very interested in health care and have been for the past eight years.

These are some domains that have spurred my curiosity and satisfied my appetite for working with ideas. They've given me a multidomain perspective. At this stage in my life, I'm not focused on the heavy lifting of running businesses, so I'm never the decider in the companies with which I'm involved. I am always the other pair of trusted eyes who advises the deciders who are running these businesses. There are also great opportunities for adaptive innovators both to actually run existing businesses and to found new ones. **With the right mindset and a passionate commitment to excel, you can be an adaptive innovator who can share in today's transformative moment, because present-day opportunities are boundless.**

An adaptive innovator of any sort works with incomplete information, especially because they are working at the edges of established domains. Adaptive innovators make decisions about things that haven't happened before. These nonlinear inflexion moments occur when a new trend emerges and is launched on a new path that moves very, very fast. You can easily be unprepared and caught off guard. That's why effectively looking ahead is so important for an adaptive innovator. When domains collide, turbulence occurs, and high-risk moments inevitably ensue. That's when you have to be flexible—willing to look at alternative ways of doing things. That's why the multiple-domain expertise is vital.

You don't necessarily have to be the person with all the needed domain expertise, but you'll need access both to it and to the best talent available, because very tricky, time-sensitive decisions have to be made, usually without complete data.

THE ADAPTIVE CORPORATION: THE KEY TO SURVIVAL AND PROSPERITY

Large incumbent corporations became successful because they learned how to scale process. But the process in which most of them have domain expertise is on the way to becoming outmoded as a result of the customer-in-control power shift we have been discussing. The future will be about the adaptive corporation—large or small, new or old. The brilliant futurist Alvin Toffler was the first to describe the adaptive corporation back in 1985. Today, that idea has become really essential for every transformative company to master.

Business leaders, whether they are entrepreneurs or large company executives, need to learn the skills of an adaptive innovator. It's what this book is about. The ability to adapt quickly is as important now as knowledge work was in an earlier time. Why? Because traditional answers and the processes that generate them have become a commodity.

Asking the right questions is much more valuable than having knowledge (knowing the right answers). In fact, computer and data science is very good at auto-answering questions, comparing and choosing from alternatives, and generating better answers without any human intervention. We actually will need *less* human intervention to do old process tasks. What computers aren't good at is making judgmental decisions. As a result, adapting by integrating expertise and making judgmental decisions in several domains in parallel will increasingly become an organization's most valuable human skill.

It is no easy task for an established corporation to make a fundamental change. Most business organizations are set up to protect their core products, not to disrupt or reinvent them. These companies empower middle management with the authority to say no, but rarely the power to say yes. They have antibodies in their culture to obstruct anything that gets in the way of continual evolution of what they've been so successful at. They become victims of their own success, and thus often misinterpret why they are successful. You can't assume that the reasons for success a decade earlier will abide as success principles today or tomorrow. The landscape changes all the time.

It's a real feat for an established company to become an adaptive corporation. A great example of a successful adaptive corporation is Starbucks. Howard Schultz built Starbucks into the largest, most successful coffeehouse retailer in the world, and stepped down in 2000. By 2008, according to David Kaplan's insightful article in *Inc.* magazine, the company had stalled and the stock price was tumbling. Howard Schultz returned to Starbucks as CEO so the company could regain its "soul." He closed 800 stores, fired most of its top executives, and refocused on delivering the kind of customer experience the old Starbucks had been so famous for. He did this by retraining his store employees and incentivizing them with health insurance, even though many were temporary workers. Now he's providing online college benefits as well. He is also at the cutting edge of technology, leveraging digital media like no other retailer. Starbucks is now booming and is expanding everywhere. Today there are approximately 1,200 Starbucks stores in China and Schultz believes there will be "north of 5,000 [there] within the next 10 years."

Howard Schultz's reinvention of Starbucks reminds me of the remarkable turnaround Steve Jobs achieved when he returned to Apple in the '90s and rebuilt it into the most valuable company in the world. Perhaps it is easier to achieve these kinds of big company transformations when the founder returns, but regardless, it isn't easy.

Companies that truly want to adapt often must begin by changing their tracking metrics. They shouldn't, of course, abandon the key financial and sales metrics that must be measured regularly. But they do need to add and give the priority to key consumer metrics like customer satisfaction, customer acquisition cost, customer retention rates, and lifetime value of a customer. The most important of these measures is customer satisfaction, and I'm a big believer in the Net Promoter Score. This is a concept developed by Fred Reichheld, Bain & Company, and Satmetrix. We'll discuss this concept in more depth later when we discuss customer experience, but the metric is simple and powerful. Sharing this metric regularly (even if the news is bad) throughout the entire organization is the first step in placing the customer at the center of the company and the signature first step in becoming an adaptive corporation.

Another example of the adaptive corporation, and perhaps the ultimate one, is Amazon. Jeff Bezos is creating the world's online market place for everything. Amazon is the looked-to model for this new era of customer marketing, with very empowered consumers who expect and get an exceptional customer experience at disruptive prices. Jeff Bezos is also an adaptive innovator. He is constantly experimenting with new services, and he adapts his model whenever he thinks he needs to in order to keep his 250 million credit-scored customers inside the Amazon ecosystem. The Fire Phone, Amazon's new smartphone, is an adaptive innovator's move to prevent Apple or Google from intervening between Jeff Bezos and his customers in the virtual point-of-sale. The Fire Phone includes a novel service that uses imaging technology to identify any product a user sees in the real world and then automatically connects the consumer with smart information and the opportunity to buy that product using Firefly technology. In addition, the Fire Phone includes "Mayday," a button that will connect a Fire Phone user to a real human being who can immediately answer a customer question. It's all part of adapting Amazon's service and continuingly moving the customer experience to a higher place.

The adaptive corporation should be viewed as a highly sophisticated system with its major mission to make its customers very, very happy.

Of course, you want to be profitable, you want to attract and retain talented people, and you want to be a good citizen in your community and have other worthy aspirations. But priority must be given to clear decider authority and accountability for systemic design decisions.

Those closest to the customer experience are best positioned to be the adaptive innovators. They are best equipped to make decisions about everything to do with an exceptional customer experience and assuring that you deliver it at the lowest cost. Adaptive innovators should be strategically placed throughout the organization to foster a dynamic, change-responsive culture and to facilitate implementation. One rule of thumb: Avoid keeping old processes just because they worked in the past and are reliable, and the organization is comfortable with them.

Here's what I might do if I were a CEO of a company wanting to become an adaptive corporation: I would take one of my most important mainstream products or services and ask a small team of my best adaptive innovators to redesign the customer experience and the customer delivery of that product or service. There would be no preconditions to the structure of the redesign—only that it must be cheaper, faster, better, and more convenient for our customers. I would fund the project to prototype this experimental alternative and see if we could improve and surpass the customer's expectation on a small scale. Unencumbered with legacy policies and overhead cost considerations, I know we would learn a lot. It's never easy to replace an old way with a new way. Why? Middle managers, as I have said, when left to their own, are always empowered to say no, and rarely empowered to say yes.

In 1997, Clayton Christensen, the much-admired Harvard Business School professor, published a groundbreaking book, *The Innovator's Dilemma*, which opened our eyes to the core issues of innovations, and our worldview has never been the same since. The dilemma he describes is the consequence of creating a disruptive new alternative. To do so, you may have to sacrifice your most valuable line of business, the core that has been the basis of your best success. Microsoft chose not to do this when it insisted that Microsoft's mobile platform had to be a derivative of its incredibly successful Windows. But Windows had been designed for PCs, where a long boot cycle was expected, supported by decades of legacy code that would use up battery power just to run the system. Apple chose to start fresh with no legacy requirements left over from the Mac. Apple designed an entirely new end-to-end system with the App Store. Google was a fast follower with Android, and decided to differentiate itself from Apple by giving the Android platform away. In contrast, Microsoft still insisted that users pay for the mobile OS, and without access to the cache of a billion mobile apps that Apple and Google have.

Christensen's inquiry addresses what is for me the central question about scaling innovation in our time: What exactly does it take to create the competence and the culture of an adaptive corporation? Competence certainly requires that a firm have the right domain expertise. Typically, this means adding new domain expertise, because innovation opportunities arise when different domains collide and change the competitive landscape. **It's rare that the innovation leader in one era is also the innovative leader in the next era.** Not impossible, as Steve Jobs proved, but not typical either. No business wants to be left out of the future—at least not in the first round of competition.

The adjustment to a new world of work is possible in existing corporations only if senior executives understand that knowledge workers and adaptive innovators are different roles requiring markedly different skills. Many knowledge workers can learn to adapt, while others never will. Existing businesses aspiring to become adaptive corporations need to commit to understanding what exactly an adaptive innovator is and how that differs from both systemic designers and knowledge workers. In the end, they will actually need conscious planning to move them from a decades-imbedded orientation of knowledge work, to a new mindset of continuous adaptive innovation centered on the customer.

2.

WHY MOONSHOTS START WITH A "NOBLE CAUSE"

Only one who devotes himself to a cause with his whole strength and soul can be a true master. For this reason mastery demands all of a person.

—Albert Einstein

Recently, I was invited with twenty other senior U.S. health care leaders to attend a private dinner meeting at the home of Dr. Patrick Soon-Shiong, the most successful health care entrepreneur. The topic for the evening was health care policy. Dr. Soon-Shiong has built a $7 billion fortune with his pioneering disruptive inventions in genomics. Having had dinner with Patrick a few months previously, I was already familiar with his breakthrough efforts.

Patrick is a genius inventor with a noble cause: to cure cancer in his lifetime. He has designated $800 million of his fortune to seed-fund a new field he terms "molecular surgery" in major technical universities around the world, including UCLA, CalTech, Stanford, MIT, and Technion in Israel. He believes that cloud computing performance is advancing with phenomenal speed. In the future, gene sequencing on a human genome will be doable in less than one minute instead of the twelve hours it takes today. When that happens, molecular surgery will enable a new era, which Patrick refers to as "precision medicine." Hospitals will monitor a cancer patient's 26,000 genes and 2 million proteins, tracking specific mutations at the molecular level, where precision medicine will have the capability to tweak these deviations with individual genes or proteins. In thirty years, Dr. Soon-Shiong says, we will look back on chemotherapy and radiology as pretty primitive cancer treatments.

Every Moonshot begins with a noble cause—a vision by the founders to make the world a better place. This is not some goal measured in terms of sales or profits. It is a higher calling. It is a mission that can make a real difference in people's lives and a cause that will rally employees, partners, investors, and beneficiaries. Almost by definition, a noble cause is hard to accomplish. It starts by making the nearly impossible, possible. Then the possible, probable. Vinod Khosla, one of Silicon Valley's greatest talents, puts it this way: "An entrepreneur is someone who dares to dream the dreams and is foolish enough to try to make those dreams come true." Guy Kawasaki was chief evangelist in the Mac group back in the early days. He reflects now: "Seize the moral high ground. It's not enough to make a great product or service—you also need to position it and explain it as a way to improve lives." Marc Andreessen is the highly respected Silicon Valley genius who embodies this story. As a twenty-two-year-old student, he got the chance to program a supercomputer at the University of Illinois. After writing the first web browser, called Mosaic, he dreamed of a noble cause that all computers should be connected to make the world better. Marc went on to cofound Netscape Communications with Jim Clark, and so began one of the most remarkable journeys ever.

Some of the best lessons I learned were from Steve Jobs and Bill Gates as I spent hours witnessing their personal dialogue. The two loved to define things into big noble causes, and they both shared an identical noble cause: to make computers personal. Empower people with personal computers and with powerful, easy-to-use software. Give people incredible personal productivity tools at an accessible price, off-the-shelf and a snap to install. Then allow people to change the world, one person at a time.

That's where the agreement between the two stopped. Bill Gates' strategy to do that was all about software. The vista he saw was all about a land grab. So he did everything possible to get everybody to use his product. That's why he invented "shrink-wrapped" software to run on personal computers.

Steve Jobs had another idea. His noble cause was that the personal computer could become a personal appliance for nontechnical people. Not just designed to crunch numbers, the PC could also be a personal media machine that would open people up to all kinds of new ideas, much the way publishing did in the Renaissance. The desktop publishing that Steve Jobs created meant that people could learn things in ways they couldn't before. Individuals were empowered to become the publishers themselves. The Macintosh system became the first successful, remarkably easy-to-use, graphics-based media machine. It offered beautiful fonts, and you could merge documents together on the screen with a point-and-click user interface. With the Mac, you could actually preview the printed page in advance of its being faithfully reproduced by the laser printer. The personal computer as a media machine became the Moonshot that changed the entire computing industry for the decades to follow.

With Bill, it was always about software and a focus on the left-brain computational power of personal computing. Steve's strategy for personal computing was about empowering the right brain of human creativity. With Steve it was also always about the complete end-to-end system. Whether it was building what later became desktop publishing, or whether it was years later when Steve came back to Apple, where he built the iPod and the iPhone, the iPad and the App Store, Steve was ever a systems designer. He thought in terms of systems that could be simplified. He constantly eliminated steps, making an elegantly simplified user experience the primary differentiator of Apple's products. The two were utilizing the same technology, but the different target Bill Gates saw was devising and advancing the dominant underlying software that everybody would want to use. He was willing to add complexity to it if it meant he could improve Microsoft's market position. On the other hand, Steve didn't care if Apple was the largest-selling computer company in the world. What he wanted was to be the *best*. He was uncompromising in product design, in how it felt to the user, how it was sold, and everything about the user experience, as we later saw with the Apple Stores that he created. End-to-end, for Steve, the store experience had to be as good as the product experience. The "Open Me First" box was totally self-explanatory, without the need to read a manual. All of these attributes were incredibly important to Steve, and they were all part of a consistent, integrated experience. He was a brilliant designer with great taste; and he was able to realize his ideas as simple, memorable notions that people could apply. Everyone knew exactly where Steve was taking the Macintosh and what he wanted to accomplish with it. Steve believed that simplification was the ultimate sophistication . . . that what you left out was more important than what you put in . . . that technology had to either be beautiful or it should be invisible.

Today, Bill Gates has an even bigger noble cause—to enhance health care and reduce extreme poverty. He has allocated much of his Microsoft wealth to create the Bill and Melinda Gates Foundation. His and Melinda's goals, among others, are to fight AIDS, tuberculosis, and malaria. He keeps giving back on a scale never seen before. He and Melinda deserve the entire world's admiration and gratitude.

I had a wonderful talk recently with my friend the renowned physician Dr. Mehmet Oz. I asked him about his noble cause. He talked about improving the world's health. He said it is not just about sending sick people to the hospital for treatment, but rather about educating people about wellness and how they can take steps to feel so much better and live longer. He said, "that is why we have to fight the battle for health in our kitchens, in our living rooms and our bedrooms and in our cars. Where we live is where the battle should be fought."

What was truly remarkable? Dr. Oz talks about a noble cause when he says, "We need to start to think of the consumer era of health and wellness and what we can do with well-care." And Wolfgang Puck, one of America's top chefs, articulates an extraordinarily consonant message when he advocates better eating. Wolfgang's noble cause also entails smarter, life-changing behavior that has positive implications on how long people live, the quality of life that they live, and even family happiness. Initially, it's astonishing—but in a pleasing way, not at all unexpected—that positive, rational visions launched from vastly different domains can be mutually supportive.

Steve Perlman, founder of Artemis Networks, is a very successful Silicon Valley serial entrepreneur and also a technology inventor genius. Our friendship extends over a quarter century. Steve invented Apple QuickTime, one of the most important technologies in every Apple product. He also cofounded WebTV and later Mova Contour software, the magical special-effects software that aged Brad Pitt backward in the movie *The Curious Case of Benjamin Button*. He has been pursuing his ambitious noble cause for ten years: to solve what many thought was an unsolvable challenge, a solution for the reality that the world is running out of wireless spectrum. Motivated by this noble cause, Steve has actually solved the problem, using physics instead of changing government policy. He calls it pCell. It's quite amazing, will change the future, and is now ready for commercial deployment.

These huge, life-changing noble causes are usually reserved for disruptive inventors and systemic designer geniuses like Steve Jobs and Jeff Bezos, who have had their own successful Moonshots. But for the rest of us, there is the possibility of becoming adaptive innovators who want to make a difference in our own smaller universes, embracing a noble cause as a powerful driving force. It can energize an organization and give both purpose and passion to the mission of the new business.

3.

WHY NOW
IS THE BEST TIME
TO BUILD
A BILLION-DOLLAR BUSINESS

Logic will get you from A to B, imagination will take you everywhere.
—Albert Einstein

This is the perfect time to build a billion-dollar business. As we discussed earlier, breathtaking technologies are now accessible to all businesses and entrepreneurs at affordable prices that are real game changers:

- Cloud computing
- Wireless sensors
- Big Data
- Mobile devices

Big Data can predict customer purchasing patterns and revolutionize everything involved in the world of selling. These four technologies are driven by bits of data, whether they be numbers, text, images, or video. The volume of these data bits is ever expanding, at exponential rates. This means that these bits will get smarter and smarter . . . and cheaper and cheaper. This is the first reason that now is the best time

38

to build a transformative business. But there are other compelling factors.

WHY NOW? ATTRACTIVE FINANCIAL INCENTIVES

The good news for economies in the West recovering from a global recession is that money-borrowing costs are low. Inflation is also very low.

Not only that, the cost of starting a business today is a fraction of what it once was. Start-ups and early-stage companies that begin as "virtual organizations" can do so with minimal payroll. Founders often take little or no pay initially, but are incentivized by the appreciation potential in founders' stock. Many other services like accounting or IT can be outsourced on a project-by-project basis at very reasonable costs. An amazing range of specialized services can be bid out online to independent contractors both here in the U.S. and abroad.

Access to capital is also improving, and in some innovative, new ways. Crowdfunding, a new financing concept, is taking off, allowing individuals to invest in early-stage companies without the high net worth traditionally required by venture capital firms. The crowdfunding platform Kickstarter is a leading example of this concept.

Another financing concept, called "shadow banking," is becoming a major factor in world finance, as the *Financial Times* recently reported in a series. Direct lending to companies by "non-banks" is replacing a sizable portion of the lending of big banks as they shed assets. The Financial Stability Board pegged the size of shadow banking at $71.2 trillion in 2012 versus $26.1 trillion a decade earlier. This represents direct lending by hedge funds, insurance companies, and crowdfunding entities.

In a recent piece in *Forbes*, Haydn Shaughnessy emphasized the auspicious "financial climate and the superabundance of capital," noting: "Bain recently reported that global aggregate financial assets will increase from $600 trillion to

$900 trillion between now and 2020. That means continued very low real interest rates for years to come." The scale of these estimates is astounding. On the one hand, economists are frustrated over the slow recovery from a world recession that almost collapsed the global economy. On the other hand, highly credible experts are pointing out that access to capital and the wealth of assets in the world is expanding at an incredible rate. My Inflexionpoint partner Shane Maine is an incredibly imaginative thinker. His recent ideas about novel ways to use credit to scale large businesses are groundbreaking. The night is darkest before the dawn, and, just when economists think the future is doomed, along comes an adaptive innovator with a new brilliant way of financing growth working capital.

THE COMING DISRUPTION OF TRADITIONAL BUSINESSES

Perhaps the most compelling reason why now is the best time ever to start a billion-dollar business is sheer business opportunity. The number and scale of these will multiply as many, if not most, traditional businesses face the reality of disruption.

We are already seeing disruptions in traditional businesses like brick-and- mortar retailers as a direct consequence of Amazon—Jeff Bezos' trailblazing vision to sell virtually everything online, at an unthinkably low price and with ever-improving customer service. Traditional book chains like Borders have already disappeared and others are seeing their businesses erode. Many more retailers will fall victim to Amazon in the future. Think, for example, of the newspaper business, which has lost readers and advertising to the Internet. Valuations for once-heralded publishing empires have plummeted as electronic publishing models have taken hold.

In my view, the present wave of disruption is just the beginning. As powerful new technologies like cloud computing and mobile devices rapidly shift power from the producer to the consumer, traditional structures will continue to unravel. The customer now has real-time access to market pricing, to more information on company websites, but even more importantly, to outspoken and frontal product reviews on the web, on Amazon and now on huge social media sites like Facebook. The trust that many brands spent years building with millions of advertising dollars can collapse overnight as new rival brands are celebrated as better, sharper-priced options.

While Amazon has already proved to be a disrupter in the publishing world, we made our own discovery when we began this book project. We met with several well-respected publishing houses, but when we learned that their business model would prevent us from getting to market for fifteen to twenty-four months, we searched for another approach. We were very fortunate to partner with Rosetta Books, a leader in e-books, which was interested in reinventing the model for hardcover book publishing. We joined forces with Ingram, a multibillion-dollar book distributor, who was also looking for a different model. Working with these two partners is allowing us to get to market at a speed unthinkable in the traditional publishing industry and without the bureaucratic management-decision layers. We are getting to the shelf in just six months, and this includes the time it has taken us to actually write most of the book. We have seen firsthand why publishing is ripe for disruption.

DISRUPTION IN HEALTH CARE

As you will see, health care—which consumes eighteen percent of the U.S. economy—is ripe for disruption, and new models are poised to redefine the industry. What makes health care a classic broken wheel among today's broken business models? First of all, the current system doesn't work very well. We spend twice as much per capita on health care as any other developed country in the world.

41

We still don't have all of our population covered with health care insurance, but we don't turn anybody away in the emergency room. So there is a way for people to get health care, even if not fully covered by health insurance. The present legacy system is so complicated and so arbitrarily regulated because it's largely defined by special interests in Washington. These governing forces have nothing to do with what would be the best way to deliver the highest-quality health care.

Many have studied Silicon Valley hoping to understand and maybe transplant its best ideas of why it has been such a source of innovation to other geographies. Silicon Valley is best understood as an ecosystem. At one level, it is thousands of independent companies and supporting resources of venture capital, lawyers, bankers, accountants, deal makers, and angel investors. At the same time, it's a living, breathing connected ecosystem that exchanges information in real time, where people move (sometimes in days from company to company) or new companies are created and older companies are acquired or go out of business in a flash. Failure, in the context of Silicon Valley, is accepted as healthy for the ecosystem and a good learning experience for the talent when it happens. No one dwells long on failure; people get past it quickly. Stuff just gets done. Very smart people came there to build new companies and accept the consequences of a decisive world. Deciders rule, frequently without consensus. Information is transparent and accountability is understood. If you aren't competent to do your job, then you are expected to move on.

Both Washington, D.C., and Silicon Valley have very smart, ambitious people and well-intentioned talent. The U.S. government's ecosystem is driven to protect special interests; Silicon Valley's ecosystem is shaped around driven entrepreneurs who are builders. They just want to build businesses to solve customer problems. These are two decidedly different models of human behavior with often-conflicting missions.

How could we ever hope to resolve, for example, the over-whelmingly complex problem of health care? The situation will never change, in my opinion, if you ask politicians to come up with the solutions. That's not what their talent is. They don't have the domain expertise to come up with such solutions, nor is it what our government is set up to do. Our government exists to make political decisions about things that the people who voted for them expect them to do. That doesn't include becoming an adaptive innovator in a massive, rapidly changing and technologically complex industry like health care.

What will drive constructive change in this complex arena of health care? I believe it will be the power shift to the consumer. For example, real-world awareness of actual costs is a powerful incentive. Once shielded from the true costs of an inefficient system, consumers are waking up to the fact that they're suddenly directly responsible for the cost of most doctor visits, which can be $125 or more. An emergency room admission can cost $750 or more. Consumers who were used to very small co-pays are now finding themselves in high-deductible plans, where the first $1,000 or more per year comes right out of their pocket. Consumers who before didn't know or care about how much a medical procedure cost now will, and that will change everything. Significant solutions to the economics of health care will come from adaptive innovators in the private sector, tackling the consequences of bad government decisions.

DISRUPTION IN EDUCATION

What about another huge American industry, higher education? Universities, some with gigantic endowments, are expanding their brick-and-mortar campuses. Harvard, for example, is adding a new campus across the Charles River from its historic center in Cambridge, Massachusetts. Harvard, perhaps the world's most valuable brand name in education, is doubling down on a second brick-and-mortar campus—despite our age's colossal changes in technology and media. Is adding new construction and overhead, at a huge investment cost, the right strategy at a time when the cost of a college education is today so high?

Universities, even with the best of reputations, resemble the most venerated corporations in this regard. Both usually succumb to their internal politics and complex cultures. So, in universities, rarely are courses ever eliminated when the curriculum is expanded . . . just like governments perpetually solve problems by adding new departments. Not surprisingly, the cost of a college education has exploded, leaving students with massive debt and often uncertain job prospects. Are graduating students—as the most relevant test—converting their diplomas into job-ready skills? Increasingly not. Sound like an industry ripe for major disruption? Few want to talk about the problem, but innovative forces in the market are already chipping away at solutions.

I was on the Board of Trustees at Brown University for seven years and on the board of overseers at the Wharton Business School for fifteen years. I served on the Board of Overseers at the MIT Media Lab for fifteen years. I've been fortunate to have firsthand experience with some really good institutions, run by extremely talented and well-intentioned people. Competence and intention are beyond question, but so many of them are crippled by the powerful forces of organizational culture.

Last winter, I made a two-hour drive through a snowstorm from New York City to Fairfield University in Connecticut, where the snowdrifts were taller than I am. It was the beginning of a wonderful experience. Father Paul Fitzgerald, president of Fairfield University, had grown up in Los Gatos, California, and was friends with many of Silicon Valley's most admired entrepreneurs, like former Apple CEO Mike Markkula and Intel's Andy Grove. Father Paul has crafted the liberal arts curriculum at Fairfield University to integrate high technology and scientific knowledge, bringing together points of view with the liberal arts in imaginative ways. His highly informed and very curious students were making intelligent connections between technology, entrepreneurship, and the liberal arts. The evening made a big impression on me, and I hope other liberal arts schools will take the time to learn from the creative curriculum of Fairfield University.

Let me return, for a moment, to Harvard . . . not to its liberal arts curriculum, but to the Harvard Business School, that part of Harvard where you would expect the most pragmatic thinking of all. One of the great education debates recently is between two top Harvard Business School professors, both of whom I personally respect, Michael Porter and Clayton Christensen. The debate is over the role of online education at the Harvard Business School.

HBX, the online business program, was designed as a credentialing adjunct for the Harvard Business School. It's intended as a bridge for people with a liberal arts education path to learn some fundamentals about accounting, financial systems, and general business. Enrollment in the online program costs about $1,500, and those who complete the course are invited to take an exam that tests whether they've satisfactorily learned the material.

My take on Michael Porter's position could be summarized this way:

> *HBX is a good adjunct to the Harvard Business School Program because we can't take what Harvard Business School does, we don't give lectures, we have discussion and debate with our students and that really needs to be a face-to-face between the professor and the students. So we're not trying to replace that, we're trying to add something to the Harvard Business School experience.*

I would characterize Clayton Christensen's opposing view this way:

> *It doesn't make enough sense because it's not disruptive enough. I forecast that in fifteen years, many of our colleges and universities are going to be bankrupt because*

they aren't facing up to the fact that many of these students are able to afford to go to these universities only if they can go on scholarship and not all schools have the ability to give scholarships, or they take on an incredible amount of student loans, which for many students is not sustainable, they can't pay it back under any reasonable term. Why? Because there isn't the same level of jobs, there isn't the wage growth; the world has changed on us.

The particular debate here is focused on whether an online course can adequately prepare a liberal arts grad for a Harvard Business School learning experience. Christensen, one of the most innovative strategists, thinks Harvard Business School should be far more aggressive than does his much-admired colleague, Porter. Imagine the excitement of these two giant intellects thinking through and considering the possible consequences of a new student experience. Time will tell, but it is clear that the customer value of a college education today in terms of cost and career preparation is very much in doubt. When the value of any industry's core product is seriously questioned, that makes it ripe for major disruption.

Another recent innovation in education is the advent of the Jack Welch Management Institute. Welch, retired CEO of General Electric and perhaps the signature management talent of his era, really understands the importance of recruiting talent, motivating talent, and giving managers greater skills to justify their promotion in an organization. He's very focused on how to construct the learning experience and says, "We do it by treating the student like a customer." That completely changes the paradigm. At his institute, the student grades the professors. What a turnabout . . . and, what's the consequence? If professors get poor grades from their customers, they get fired. What a big . . . no, EXPLOSIVE idea!

Go one step further. Imagine if you said to the government,

let's treat citizens like customers. As you stand in line to re-new your driver's license or as you try to call the IRS to ask a question, does anyone think that government cares at all about how the customers feel? What if the services we are getting from government aren't appreciated by the custom-ers: Should we (the customers) get to fire the services by rating their performance? In a way, the Arab Spring revolt that began in late December 2010 was a dramatic manifes-tation of this attitude. In more stable parts of the world, there can be good reason to moderate how drastically change occurs. But we also need to be aware that, in a social media–saturated world, the pressure for urgent, straight-forward customer-driven change will be increasingly hard to thwart.

If you believe in empowering customers, then patients can be customers … students can be customers … and even citizens can be customers. If you start considering each of these groups as customers, they will increasingly presume their right to vote on the customer experience. If they don't like it, they can fire the provider, be it a doctor, a teacher, or even a government official. And it's all about voting on the quality of the service offered: "It's not that we don't want the service," they may be saying, "but we want it in a cheaper, faster, better way."

No industry that deals with customers is safe from dis-ruption in the future, in my opinion. This opens up huge, unprecedented opportunities for adaptive innovators to create exciting, new substantial businesses. Those new businesses will suck oxygen out of existing industries. That means traditional corporations need to carefully think through the implications of this power shift from producers to customers. They need to become adaptive corporations, with a culture that genuinely embraces and exploits innova-tions that matter to the customers they serve.

Despite all the problems we hear about in our news me-dia every day, I believe this is the best time in history to build a billion-dollar business. Those adaptive innovators and adaptive corporations that seize the moment, in my opinion, have boundless opportunities.

In the next section, I discuss the huge changes affecting the middle classes in America and abroad today and into the future. These middle-class consumers represent the exciting core of unprecedented future demand.

PART II

HUGE CHANGES TO THE MIDDLE CLASS

1.

WHAT'S REALLY
GOING ON IN THE U.S.?

As soon as tradition has come to be
recognized as tradition, it is dead.
                    —Allan Bloom,
                        philosopher and academician

A lot of people assume that America was always built on a middle class. It actually wasn't. That's really a post–World War II development. America's middle class has only been around for roughly sixty years, and I've been able to watch it evolve during my lifetime.

I was a little kid when World War II ended in 1945. With factories tooled up to make tanks, jeeps, and transport trucks, cars for personal use just weren't built during the war, and gas was rationed. But that quickly changed. We were living in New York City at the time and, in 1948, a few years after my brothers, Arthur and David, were born, we moved out to a small town in Long Island called St. James, about fifty miles from the city. I can still remember the first time my father drove us from St. James to Smithtown, which was only four miles away. I don't think I'd ever been there before, and my parents hadn't been there since before the war. It was a pretty big deal.

I remember going to a Jewish clothing store called Schechter's. We didn't buy new clothes very often; "hand-me-downs" were how youngsters had many of their clothing needs outfitted. That, too, made a shopping trip another big deal. I can remember Mr. Schechter's daughter, a very nice young woman who was deaf, reading our lips and using sign language to speak with her family. Merchandise was stacked to a high ceiling, and she mastered using a tool called a pick stick, a hand mechanical grabber, to lift a box of shoes off a high shelf. If you were lucky, a clothes-shopping outing might include a visit to the Smithtown movie theater for two features with a twenty-five cent admission plus five cents for the popcorn.

No one had a television at home. But there was a TV at a restaurant in nearby Stony Brook called The Three Village Inn. I would go there on weekends with Dad. His friends would all sit around, nursing their Rheingold beers and squinting at a football game on a Philco TV set with a tiny screen—all of seven inches, measured diagonally! Uninterested in the broadcast, I would wander into the adjacent antique store and rummage through their secondhand stuff, intrigued by any of the mechanical gadgetry.

In 1949, Dad bought one of the first television sets for consumers, and we could watch a GE ten-inch black-and-white TV in our own living room. Our neighbors seemed amazed, even when the stations were just broadcasting test patterns during daytime. During the month of June, it was typical for television waves to reflect off of the ionosphere during what the ham radio world terms "sky wave sporadic propagation." As a hobbyist, I loved chasing DX signals, as they were called, from distant televisions stations hundreds of miles away, transmitting their routine television programs. In 1950, there was no network television and in fact during most of the daytime, TV stations transmitted only television test patterns.

In the main, ours was a very simple world. Our unpaved dirt roads were clogged with mud after rainstorms. We rode bicycles to get around. There were no organized activities for people, especially youngsters. Kids took care of themselves, and I hung out with forerunners of today's geeks. This was farm country, and the most important local person was Vincent the farmer, who planted hundreds of acres in corn and potatoes—including some of our fields. I went to school in a one-room building. This was before the advent of housing developments and shopping malls. The notion of a middle class never even occurred to us. Nor did people score themselves on the value or number of possessions they owned.

The fabled middle class didn't arise until a series of transformative events after the Second World War. GIs came back, they formed families, and had children during the late 1940s and early '50s. The GI Bill gave these veterans free college tuition. In companies, employer-paid, tax-free health insurance became a standard job benefit. With just a high school education, you could get a job that would lead to a career, usually with the same organization for your entire working lifetime. Medium-level skills earned high enough pay that you could live a very comfortable lifestyle.

The American suburban model followed soon thereafter, and created a stage set for this fleeting period in American history. Even today, it really exists only in the United States. A huge number of kids were born, the "Baby Boomers," and the rapidly expanding families they populated needed housing and schools. In 1956, the Eisenhower administration was able to have Congress pass the Federal-Aid Highway Act, which built the Interstate Highway System as a safeguard to protect our missiles from the Soviets. As a derivative effect, this transportation network reinforced the nation's new suburban topography and opened America to a new age of growth. This expansion vastly extended both our occupational direction and our residential sprawl.

At the same time, other American infrastructures blossomed, including vastly improved telephone systems and the electronic communications of television networks that enabled far more sophisticated mass marketing to consumers. In tandem with suburban expansion, America's infrastructure supported the largest homogenous market in the world, geographically protected by oceans to the east and west and cushioned by friendly neighbors, Canada to the north and Mexico to the south. Geographically, the suburbanized U.S. couldn't have happened in a better place or at a better time.

Model American families were portrayed on television with shows like *Father Knows Best* and *The Adventures of Ozzie and Harriet*. Although this seemingly content and stable world was regarded as a long-standing American norm, it was actually just a brief and very fragile interlude in the American experience. In the 1960s, fast-food restaurant chains, home freezers, and, soon after, microwave foods began to alter the dynamics of family life. Woodstock and The Pill for birth control, along with other changes, redefined the traditional nuclear family. The times were turbulent. The assassinations of President Kennedy and the Rev. Martin Luther King were a terrible shock to America, as was the unpopular Vietnam War.

In the 1970s, new opportunities encouraged women to enter the workforce in droves, resulting in an explosion of two-income households. The rapidly spreading dual-income families of the 1970s advanced middle-class earning power. **Armed with discretionary income, a consumption-centered economy was born, built around a consumer-spending nucleus with about seventy percent of GDP coming from that sector.** Such an economic structure was unique in the world. No other economy in history had a seventy percent consumer-spending nucleus or as liberal use of natural resources. America's economic clout skyrocketed. This new middle class was built on high-paying jobs, particularly white-collar jobs where employment with the same company for life seemed secure. Home ownership was made accessible with mortgages. Cars were purchased with low down payments, and the emergence of credit cards encouraged Americans to shop frequently. With only about five percent of the world's population, we were twenty-five percent of the world's economy! And we devoured resources like oil, coal, gas, and water at a much faster rate per capita than any other society in the world.

During the 1980s, the Moonshot arrival of the personal computer had a significant effect on business productivity. It allowed companies to forecast and track important metrics in a way they never could before. Profit margins expanded while U.S. corporations expanded their businesses to promising new markets abroad. The stock market soared during this decade. And the middle class continued to expand.

By the mid-1990s, the Moonshot of the World Wide Web arrived. Now communication was transformed, particularly with the advent of email, leading to a further important advance in productivity.

Throughout this postwar boom, America's middle class was enjoying an ever more opulent lifestyle. And an element of the "conspicuous consumption" life, with fancy cars and huge mansions previously available only to celebrities and the wealthy, began to creep into middle-class expectations. Houses got larger, even though family sizes decreased. Kitchens were remodeled, pools were added, and everyone of driving age had a car. Color TVs were to be found in room after room of a typical home. Even as success was measured more and more by the number and worth of one's possessions, ownership of these conspicuous possessions was increasingly built around debt.

THE CRASH OF 2008 EXPOSED AMERICA'S MIDDLE CLASS

The Crash of 2008 was devastating. The post–World War II American bubble burst. When the Great Recession hit, Americans were way overleveraged with credit card debt and upside-down home mortgages. After the recession ended, workers discovered that the days of secure, middle-skilled, high-paying jobs were over. Automation, globalization, and computer productivity had eliminated millions of working jobs done the old-fashioned way. Conspicuous consumption—far more a figment of marketing imagery than a normative behavior—collapsed and is now is a luxury affordable to just a small percentage of families at the top of the economic pyramid.

In April 2014, an Associated Press article in *USA Today* observed: "nearly five years after the Great Recession ended, more people are coming to the painful realization that they're no longer part of [the middle class]. They are former professionals now stocking shelves at grocery stores, retirees struggling with rising costs and people working part-time jobs but desperate for full-time pay."

The article goes on to cite some stunning numbers:

> *Since 2008, the number of Americans who call themselves middle class has fallen by nearly a fifth, according to a survey in January by the Pew Research Center, from 53% to 44%. Forty percent now identify as either lower-middle or lower class compared with just 25% in February 2008.*
>
> ***According to Gallup, the percentage of Americans who say they're middle or upper-middle class fell 8 points between 2008 and 2012, to 55%.*** *. . . . The difference between the income earned by the wealthiest 5% of Americans and by a median-income household has risen 24% in 30 years, according to the Census Bureau.* [Emphasis added.]

Being pessimistic isn't in my nature. The changes taking place in the world of work are profound and irreversible. I believe with equal strength that the underlying scenario I'm describing in *Moonshot!* can prove to be as stunningly positive as it is dramatic. The outcome rests on how much ingenuity we are willing to add. If we don't do the ingenious ourselves, others in the world will.

The inescapable, central fact is that our lifestyle and the fabric of our society are changing because of an underlying transformation in the structure of work worldwide. One result: More Americans want a middle-class lifestyle than jobs exist for people to earn at a middle-class level, at least to the consumption standard that the U.S. middle class has become accustomed. In broad measure, a satisfactory standard of consumption needs to be available to more and more people at much lower price points than what we've known in the past. This is happening right now with companies like Amazon, which are providing a huge selection of products at disruptive prices. I believe that while the conspicuous consumption middle-class lifestyle is unsustainable, an adaptive middle class will emerge who will enjoy a more modest lifestyle enabled by the arrival of exponential technologies, and the exciting new businesses created around them.[2]

AT THE HEART OF TODAY'S UPHEAVAL: THE REDEFINED WORLD OF WORK

An incredible irony now faces the knowledge-worker-led middle class that enabled the economic efficiencies and many of the technological advances that now shape future realities: What has happened to the same highly skilled, white-collar, middle managers who readily adopted productivity tools like personal computers and the Internet over the past twenty years? They are now at risk of becoming casualties in our new economy. Potentially, they face the same fate that a previous generation of mid-skilled, high school graduates experienced decades earlier. Why? **Increasingly automation and expert systems are able to perform a lot of what middle managers once did well. Cheaper, faster, better, and more convenient ways now exist to get done what earlier was middle-management work.** Life isn't fair. But at least, in the U.S. we all have options if we take the initiative to adapt.

White-collar jobs, where the skills were acquired through training programs and refined through promotion in organizations and work in growing companies, are disappearing. Many young people are attempting to enter the job market with a liberal arts college education that is totally unconnected with the work that businesses need to have done. Today's world demands that workers have the skills to be job-ready.

In recent decades, an increasingly important aspect of work has been the personalization or specified tailoring of mass-produced product. As machines and manufacturing processes became better able to reliably produce manufactured components, human work was invested higher up the value chain making judgmental decisions to tailor goods and services.

The only answer to new job creation in the U.S., I believe, will come from adaptive innovators or the businesses they create. It's not *one* of the answers, it's the *only* answer, because both public- and private-sector jobs are steadily being eliminated to meet the expenses imposed by nonproductive outlays like covering pensions and their related health care costs. A June 2014 article in *The Economist* drove home the point: "According to a study from Oxford University, 47% of occupations are at risk of being automated in the next few decades. As innovation wipes out some jobs and changes others, people will need to top up their human capital throughout their lives."

The 1980s empowered the individual knowledge worker with personal productivity tools. The 1990s empowered organizations with the Internet, outsourcing, and globalization. Early twenty-first century cloud innovations, Big Data, and the advent of mobile technology mean that work productivity will improve without the need for many of these employees. The future of work will couple continuing declines in the cost of enabling technology with a heightened value for domain experts with a comprehensive command of specialized areas. Work will be conducted more and more in collaborative project teams focused directly on the customer. And these teams will comprise greater numbers of women, as approximately sixty percent of college students now are women.

Evolving business models are organized around defined projects that are bid out to their virtual ecosystems of independent contractors, a labor force that I will later address in terms of the evolving "free-agent" economy. Where will all these displaced middle managers go? Many will become independent consultants contracting their services as skilled project managers and project contributors over a virtual, web-based labor market. Many will work out of their homes, and some will join start-ups or rapidly growing small companies. LinkedIn, for example, with over 300 million members worldwide, is a key enabler for the free-agent nation.

A rapidly expanding and relatively stable and peaceful international environment also paved the way for a globalized economy. As high-paying middle-class jobs are vanishing in the U.S., so have secure career paths to retirement. That is occurring just as modern medicine and lifestyle awareness have substantially increased lifespans. While eighty-eight percent of Americans today may have a high school education, this group can certainly no longer expect to live a middle-class lifestyle similar to their parents' generation.

THE NEW ADAPTIVE MIDDLE CLASS

In the U.S., we have a very pragmatic culture, and I suspect that the vast majority of us will learn to become members of an adaptive middle class far more easily than we might expect. The Millennial generation is, I believe, destined to lead the way. They have a nearly inborn skepticism that's supported by the instantly available information flow of social media channels. They check out products and services automatically, looking opinions up on the web to see what other people have to say. Usually, they will get interested only if other customers said a particular product or service was a good deal. Their product purchasing decisions are nearly untouched by conventional advertising. They're driven by the assessments on Yelp, Rotten Tomatoes, the product reviews on Amazon, and other social media.

The Millennials have different aspirations than their parents. They've already figured out they're unlikely to experience an improvement over their parents. They're the first generation since the Second World War that didn't naturally expect to have a better economic life than their parents did. For example, they are saving at higher rates than older generations. And they're thinking about life differently. They are increasingly moving into cities. They view renting an apartment or a smaller house as a viable alternative to yesterday's "big-buy" mindset. Instead of owning cars, many will realistically adapt to the need to rent peer-to-peer mobility through services like Lyft and Uber. They'll be pleased to arrange an affordable vacation through Airbnb.

This new adaptive middle class will require affordable products and services that are in many cases differing from much of what is available today. This will open up incredible opportunities for adaptive innovators to develop exciting new businesses. It also will provide many traditional companies, adaptive corporations, a good chance to reinvent their products to appeal to these new middle-class requirements.

2.

THE EXPLODING MIDDLE CLASS
IN EMERGING MARKETS

With lower start-up costs and a vastly expanded market for online services, the result is a global economy that for the first time will be fully digitally wired—the dream of every cyber-visionary of the early 1990s, finally delivered, a full generation later.

> —Marc Andreessen,
> cofounder of Netscape Communications
> and cofounder and general partner of
> Andreessen Horowitz

By 2020, approximately sixty-five percent of the world's GDP economic growth will be coming from emerging markets. In 2013, emerging markets' share of world economic growth passed that of developed countries at fifty-two percent, moving up from a forty-eight percent share of growth the preceding year. A new metric called E2E trade—direct commerce between emerging economies like India and China—is skyrocketing, and we in the West are hardly aware of it!

The new middle class in global emerging markets will be gigantic. It is expected to reach more than two billion people by 2020. Their incomes will range from the equivalent of $4,000 per year up to $30,000. This ascending global middle class has aspirations that are far more frugal than have been the hallmarks of the American Dream. Instead of a 3,000-square-foot house in the suburbs, it's an 800-square-foot high-rise apartment. Instead of a $40,000 automobile, it may be a motorcycle or an automobile priced under $10,000. It's not an international brand of smartphone costing $700 to $800, but one that may cost $200 or less. Remember, there is no carrier funding to subsidize phone hardware prices as in the U.S.

The new middle class lodged in the high-rises of Mumbai, Shanghai, Guangzhou, and Kuala Lumpur are the rising class of workers driving those frugal automobiles and routing data through those sharply priced smartphones. U.S. and British ex-pats used to be running multinational companies everywhere in Asia. Not so much anymore. Overseas managers are increasingly highly educated, multilingual Asians. They have taken U.S. and Western commercial ideas and adapted them to the larger and faster-growing Asian markets.

Asia has an increasingly better-educated population, forming the core of the emerging middle class. They have the skills that actually enable them to earn money at better-paying jobs. It's very realistic to expect that these higher-skilled jobs will increasingly be done worldwide by people who already have the needed skills. That's a challenge for the U.S. in particular, because we have many people in the bottom fifty percent of our middle class who don't have world-class skills. We're focused on getting people to be literate and able to do simple math. While we have the best higher education system in the world, it's getting harder and harder for U.S. Millennials to get jobs even if they have college educations. In fact, many of the Millennials aren't getting what we consider a college-educated person's salary. They're often going into the kinds of jobs that someone in the past would have settled for if they came right out of high school—*if* they can even get a job. Increasingly it's irrelevant *where* work is performed. The relevant criterion today is the skill level to do the work at all. In so many situations today, work can be performed by highly educated individuals in the emerging economies by workers who are job-ready. Their labor is available often at a fraction of the cost charged by domestic U.S. competitors, with their work transmitted electronically instantly and at nearly no cost.

The Republic of Korea—South Korea—is worth mentioning for comparison with the United States. A nation of 50 million, South Korea is a marvel of technological innovation. Educational attainment in Korea is astonishing, and not just in math and the tech sciences, but across the board in cognitive skills, even surpassing Singapore in a 2014 Pearson report. The focus on education is so strong that a network of private *hagwons*—academies and tutors—supplements formal education and is available 24/7. There are an estimated 100,000 *hagwons* in South Korea, and seventy-five percent of Korean children attend them. Sixty-five percent of Koreans hold some sort of college degree—the highest level in the OECD, and, as you might imagine, the job relevance of the degrees is decidedly more pragmatic than in the U.S.

The Asian success story has now spread to Eastern Europe, the Middle East, Africa, and Latin America. One after another, nations throughout the world are flexing economic strengths that the U.S. would do well to study and often to emulate. When I've gone to Turkey, I see that a very small number of families own the businesses in every industry. It's not a middle-class ownership country. But Turkey's new entrepreneurs, known as the Anatolian Tigers, headed by conservative, religious, and self-made men from Anatolia, have led the way into new markets in the Middle East, Central Asia, and Africa. Turkey has a government that believes its mission is to aggressively expand bilateral trade. It's constantly leading business promotion groups to different parts of the emerging-market world. It turns out that Turkish television soap operas are very popular with all kinds of audiences in emerging markets. This transition is a great image builder for the Turks. As soon as the U.S. military moves out, the Turkish entrepreneurs move in.

My brother Arthur, who is a senior fellow at Tufts University's Fletcher School Council for Emerging Market

Enterprises, has verified these observations about Turkey: Who was the first group of businessmen to go into Libya after the government fell? It was from Turkey. Who was the first group to go into northern Iraq? It was the Turks. Afghanistan? It was the Chinese and Turks. The first to go into Africa to expand trade there? It was China, Turkey, India, and Brazil. A country's competitive positioning in the new world of work is influenced by many factors: Clear goal-setting and the aggressive pursuit of trade opportunities must rank as two of the most formidable.

While Americans rue the middle class they see slipping away, a new middle class is arising in the world's emerging economies, driven by their own ambitions and vision. Throughout the world, and especially in emerging markets, a different ideal of the middle-class dream is arising. Instead of copying the American middle-class lifestyle model heralded in Hollywood's films and TV, emerging economies are building their own alternative model, grounded on frugal products and services at disruptive pricing compared to the norms we're used to. And the new middle class in emerging markets represents an unprecedented source of demand for new products and services for adaptive innovators to target.

CHINA ON THE MOVE

In the "Arabian Nights" tales, a humble woodcutter named Ali Baba unravels the code of the forty thieves' den by uttering the words "Open Sesame." Ali Baba's reward: He gets to keep the loot. When a Chinese entrepreneur picked the name, it was because he thought the story was known throughout the world. In a 2014 *Business Insider* piece, he also noted, "We also registered the name Alimama, in case someone wants to marry us!'"

Alibaba is poised for a gigantic IPO valuing the company at well over $100 billion and perhaps closer to $200 billion, well ahead of Facebook's record-breaker. Born in 1964, Jack Ma, Alibaba's founder, started out as a $15-a-month English teacher. Intent on learning the English language's conversational nuances, he had spent his student days hanging out at a Hangzhou hotel with a steady stream of foreign visitors. In fifteen years, Alibaba has grown to be twice the size of Amazon and has 231 million active buyers. Its present transaction volume is larger than that of Amazon and eBay combined and accounts for more than eighty percent of all the online shopping in China. More than sixty percent of all the package deliveries in China come from Alibaba sites, and the firm is as active in Internet content and payment strategies as it is in merchandising.

Alibaba is also, to an important extent, a mirror of the transition that is taking place within China itself. China's President Xi has already declared the goal of creating a balance between the export economy of China being the world's factory and the nation's steadily growing significance as a domestic consumption economy. How is this transition being realized? A massive migration is under way from the farms to the cities. This transformation is taking place at unprecedented speed. According to *Bloomberg Business Week*, "In 1978 there were no Chinese cities with more than 10 million people and only two with 5 million to 10 million; by 2010, six cities had more than 10 million and ten had from 5 million to 10 million. By the following year, a majority of Chinese were living in urban areas for the first time in the country's history." A byproduct of urban migration has been the sale of farm property. The newly developed banking system has been designed to accommodate this influx of capital and equity. In the past, people saved money because there were neither health insurance protections for a rainy day nor retirement programs. Gradually these are being instituted. And people are more willing to loosen their purse strings. Economic stimulus is increasingly aimed at balancing domestically driven consumer spending with the already strong export economy.

The recently eased one-child-per-family policy has now led to fewer workers competing for jobs. So China is no longer the low-cost factory for the world, and China's President

Xi has told the population that they must begin to adapt to a different economic model, in which its people will be making more money in higher-skilled jobs. China may not be a democracy, but the Chinese are just as capitalist as we are. China may lack a developed rule of law, but the Chinese system is getting a little bit closer to it. They don't have a fully functioning banking system, but they're moving in that direction. The Chinese are trying to clean up corruption, and their leaders are slowly shifting lending policy toward the private sector.

A NEW INDIA

In India, the new prime minister, Narendra Modi, is leader of the BJP Party and a Hindu Nationalist who earlier headed India's Gujarat state. Assuming office in May 2014, Modi and the BJP wrested power from the Indian National Congress party—long the dominant political force in India. The international business community has high expectations that Modi will lead India toward more internationally open and less insider-corrupt policies, especially in the banking community and in reducing constraints on foreign investment. What happens inside the domestic India economy now has noteworthy consequences in the West, where we are learning to appreciate the magnitude of even small percentage shifts in the mammoth economies of China and India. With India's huge population of 1.2 billion, the base of scale is so great that a single percentage point swing in increasing GDP or in decreasing the impact of bureaucracy or corruption is massive.

I'm involved with a new mobile business targeting the youth of India's emerging middle class. My Inflexionpoint Asia partner Neeraj Chauhan is a superb operating executive and has assembled an excellent team to run Obi - Connect Smarter, our new smartphone firm for emerging markets. Along with Neeraj Chauhan, we recruited experienced mobile executive Ajay Sharma as Obi India CEO.

Obi - Connect Smarter's primary product is called Obi Octopus 8, a high-end 8-core smartphone with Connect Smarter services especially designed for teens and young adults. Its differentiated creative offering will include lots of youth content, such as cricket scores and Bollywood entertainment. The device will also be localized into several of India's distinctive languages that vary across the different Indian states. "Obi kids" have never known a world that wasn't mobile; and they rarely make voice calls, preferring to text with one another even when they are in the same room. Our prices will start as low as USD $80 and range to $220. The business model will operate with a very lean organization using partnering relationships. Since Obi - Connect Smarter is a private company and very lean, we can be more price-disruptive than most international public companies.

When we founded Obi, we asked ourselves: "If eighty percent of the smartphones sold in India are under USD $220, is it possible to build a profitable company that offered a very high-quality mobile device *and* bundled services that would be nearly as good as Samsung and iPhone?" We think the answer is yes, if we simply lag the big brands' high tech by about a few months. Technology is commoditizing so quickly that differentiation can come through fashion design of the device and our various bundled services. In Obi's case, we hope to build an international brand and take advantage of our team's domain expertise with supply chain, distribution, sales channels, frugal expense management, and big-brand consumer marketing. Early-adopter customers tolerate premium prices for the latest high-tech devices, offsetting R&D amortization and covering very expensive marketing campaigns. However, slightly older technology commands an equally attractive market position. For example, when it was first introduced, the iPhone 4S was considered a superb product. It's been replaced by the latest and greatest, 5S. But we can build a product better than the 4S today and sell it profitably for a round $100. And we will bundle in the latest services so our market doesn't feel they are buying yesterday's newspaper. We are also responding to a particular market condition in India. Markets like India are unique versus the U.S., because carriers don't subsidize mobile devices with two-year contracts as they do in the U.S. At this disruptive price point, younger consumers—in the high teens up to maybe the high twenties—are a huge market. The smartphone market growth in India alone in 2013 was up 180 percent; about 257 million feature phones and smartphones were sold last year. The market overall is growing almost thirty percent a year.

Obi - Connect Smarter's profile is the classic model for the frugal middle class at the center of emerging markets:

- It has big market growth opportunity, especially among youth between sixteen and twenty-eight years old.
- Disruptive pricing is key because young people want the best but can't afford the premium prices of Apple and high-end Samsung smartphones.
- But there can be no compromise in the quality of the product. And there's no reason to compromise, because hardware components are just a commodity.

It may not be quite the fully-featured products that could be bought at the high end, but it is still a very, very attractive value and quality experience at the price points, positioned a bit higher than street-vendor prices and dramatically lower than the well-known global brands.

Why wouldn't someone like Nokia come in and compete with us? They can, to a point. Microsoft added about 32,000 new employees when it acquired Nokia's mobile business. They are strategically disadvantaged, when we can offer the same quality products with only a few hundred employees. In fact, Microsoft announced in mid-July 2014 that it was lay-ing off 18,000 workers, *most of them from Nokia.*

Here's a dramatic example of the new reality: **New com-panies are being built without having to replicate the entire infrastructure of the companies that they're** trying to replace. Amazon demonstrated this when they didn't have to create a huge middle management in order to build a massive customer-experience business online, even while they invested in large supply centers to have same-day delivery. The once prized middle management of traditional companies is a huge disadvantage matched by the lower-cost technology used by disruptors.

Disruptive pricing is a fundamental opportunity, I believe, in industry after industry—whether in the developed world or the emerging-market world—and it's all part of the reinvention of the term middle class. A hard company for us to compete with will be the Chinese success story Xiaomi. It makes good quality mobile products, and is an expert marketer over the Internet. It's had excellent success with its flash sales campaigns, most recently selling 100,000 smartphones over the Internet in China in just ninety seconds. Xiaomi has intentions to become a global, emerging-markets brand, and we assume it will be successful.

The global emerging market is so large that we are hoping to succeed, even assuming Xiaomi will be successful too. What differentiation do we have over Xiaomi? While Xiaomi is expert at online marketing, we already own an IT distributor business in India, and we can sell to the mom-and-pop retail stores in smaller cities, too.

THE EMERGING MIDDLE CLASS IN THE FUTURE

Thomas Friedman's landmark book on globalization, *The World Is Flat*, appeared in 2005, nearly a decade ago. Tom did a remarkable job of capturing a world centered on changes in producer economics. Not surprisingly, Walmart is celebrated in *The World Is Flat* for its mastery of "supply-chaining." Walmart was really the last chapter in a West-based, production-centered world. Amazon and Alibaba mark the transition to a customer-centric world, enabled by modern technology and reflective of both new streams of personal income and new pressures to optimize spending for the best possible returns. Now the story isn't just about Asian exports to the West, but about consumption in these emerging economies, especially those in Asia.

The new middle-class populations of these emerging countries—in aggregate, more than two billion people— are much better educated than they were when globalization first got under way in the 1980s and '90s. The dynamics within these markets are also shifting dramatically, as production moves from China to new manufacturing centers in places like the Philippines, Thailand, Vietnam, and Malaysia. The global economy has lived up to most of the expectations set by visionary thinkers like Tom Friedman, but the game has now shifted to a different stage. **The customer emerging in the new middle class will set the foundation for the entire middle-class experience around the world.**

Aware of the trappings of a better life for decades, shifts in the world of work and capital have now given these markets—including markets in Asia, Africa, the Middle East, Latin America, and Eastern Europe—discretionary spending money. Because of communications, these populations are well aware of the kinds of products and services that we've had for a long time in the West, but it requires a new, affordable model to bring them price-point alternatives that their incomes and wealth will both allow and motivate them to buy. As I have said, in many countries, the people in the new emerging middle class have been saving for years because their homelands typically have neither health insurance nor retirement planning. People have had to save for a rainy day, and that's a behavior that's been baked into their mindset.

In a decade, China and India will be very different countries from what they are today. And you can't understand emerging markets by thinking of them in a generic way. They must be appreciated country by country, culture by culture. Thailand, for example, has been in the deep turmoil of transition. Indonesia has suffered from corruption and just had a government change. As the largest Muslim country in the world, Indonesia has new leadership guiding its potential. Malaysia's path has been slower, but possibilities are emerging. Obviously, Singapore is incredibly important. Vietnam, although still a Communist country, has growing capitalist practices and extraordinary technical talent. Misfit, one of the companies in Silicon Valley I'm involved with, has sixty data scientists in Vietnam who are working on predictive analytics for mobile devices. We do a lot of our research in Vietnam. Why? While the country ranks fifty-seventh economically in the world, it's one of the top twenty nations in mathematics skills.

Of course, a lot of Western brands have been transplanted to these markets. One of the most popular brands in China is Buick, owned by General Motors, marketed as a luxury car. Such American staples as Pizza Hut and KFC are also big success stories in China. But for the most part, more and more indigenous companies will develop. Until now, the majority of managers were American ex-pats or aliens trained in the States. Now, emerging markets have the skills and don't need U.S. ex-pats as much, making them a dying breed. Why pay exorbitant allowances to locate people abroad who aren't assimilated with the local culture? Across the globe—including in the United States—the ability to adapt businesses innovatively will require an intimate knowledge of what works within each particular culture.

For a developed-economy firm to successfully penetrate emerging markets and score well with the emerging middle class demands the most imaginative sort of adaptive thinking. In 2010, McKinsey published a study titled *Capturing the World's Emerging Middle Class*. It urged "'scale at speed' approaches to penetrate the developing world's increasingly prosperous consumer markets." For example, the study cites:

- Brewer SABMiller had to adjust ingredients to match acceptable market price points, substituting locally supplied cassava and sugar rather than barley and maize.

- LG, the consumer electronics manufacturer, "has found that people in many developing markets are more willing to pay for better service than are their counterparts in the developed world. The company launched a premium offering that not only gives consumers a full-time contact person who acts as a go-between with LG and monitors the health of products but also guarantees maintenance visits within 6 hours (compared with the normal 24-hour commitment)."

The Spanish-based fashion retailer Zara has done a masterful job of configuring itself for a global market, becoming the world's largest apparel retailer. A 2009 *New York Times* article on the "Frugal Fashionista" reported "that Zara needs just two weeks to develop a new product and get it to stores, compared to the six-month industry average, and launches around 10,000 new designs each year." Eyeball Zara's April 2014 store count, and you will note a presence in eighty-eight countries, including fifty-eight in Mexico, forty-six in Brazil, seventy-one in Russia, forty-four in Poland, and twenty-two in Romania. A 2012 *Business Insider* article on Zara noted: "Another important way that Zara has impacted the fashion is by negating the idea that expensive clothes are more desirable. Kate Middleton [today the Duchess of Cambridge, of course] has often been photographed wearing the brand, and getting something chic for a steal is something to brag about." Samsonite—a middle-market mainstay luggage brand in the United States—has had positive response in positioning itself as a luxury brand in China and is now pursuing a comparable course in India.

The rise of a frugal middle class in emerging markets is opening substantial opportunities for local and neighboring adaptive innovators to meet their demands for new products and services. The question is whether Western companies, particularly adaptive corporations, will participate to their full potential in this huge new market.

PART III

HOW TO CREATE A BILLION-DOLLAR BUSINESS CONCEPT

1.

INTRODUCTION

*The purpose of a business is to
create a customer.*
          —Peter F. Drucker,
               management expert

There are two types of transformative businesses. The first involves innovating within existing industries like consumer retail, health care, or education. This is by far the most common source of new business development and the area which I am addressing in *Moonshot!*. The second type of transformative business is even more ambitious and involves inventing a whole new industry. This is what Mark Zuckerberg did, for example, when he created Facebook, the leader in social media around the world.

Moonshot! is aimed at adaptive innovators and adaptive corporations intent on transforming an existing industry or a part of an industry with a much better product or service as seen through the customer's eyes. As we will discuss later, appropriate domain expertise is essential, as is thorough research on current competitors, their business models, the underlying economic models, and how their customers view their products and services—the good and the bad.

Any team aspiring to transform a business concept must be well versed in the four exponential technologies I discussed in Section I: Cloud computing, wireless sensors, Big Data, and smart mobile devices. It is hard to imagine a transformative business strategy today that must not, for example, embrace mobile devices. These are the most important communications instruments in the world today, connecting everyone to real-time information, news, sports, entertainment, and e-commerce products, among others.

Creating a billion-dollar business concept is a collaborative process with fact-based information and a launch team (usually at least two founders) who can brainstorm in an open-minded atmosphere. **A Moonshot-inspired transformational company must have more than just a Big Idea. The concept must be as possible to deliver and as potentially viable economically as it would be transformative from the customer's viewpoint.** This is the foundation of a business model. The next step is to determine what it takes to move from the possible to the probable. This section presents four approaches in creating a billion-dollar business concept:

- Solve a Billion-Dollar Problem
- Relentless Pursuit of "There Has to Be a Better Way"
- Disruptive Pricing
- Deliver a Lights-Out Customer Experience

2.

SOLVE A BILLION-DOLLAR PROBLEM

We never sat around and theorized.
We just started building.

> —Julia Hartz,
> cofounder and president,
> Eventbrite

The simple answer to building a billion-dollar concept is to solve a billion-dollar problem . . . and to solve it in a much better way than anyone has ever done before.

After I was appointed marketing VP for Pepsi-Cola Company in 1970, my first assignment was to help design a small glass soft-drink bottle so Pepsi could better compete against Coke's very distinctive and popular 6.5-ounce glass bottle. In those days, Pepsi had not done much market research. So we decided to conduct a baseline, quantitative in-home use test to observe how consumers were consuming carbonated beverages. The test was designed so that we delivered a carton of returnable glass bottles of soda to 550 homes every week and gave consumers the choice as to which soft drinks we left with them. After nine weeks, we saw a really interesting pattern: No matter how much beverage we left the previous week, the household inventory was always empty when we returned the following week.

We asked ourselves what turned out to be a really important question: Why were we trying to design a better *small* Pepsi bottle when the real opportunity was to create a *very large* bottle? Pepsi made its profits by how many ounces of beverage a family consumed each week.

Within twelve months, working with DuPont, we had developed a large two-liter plastic bottle. Coincidently, new consumer sales channels, in the form of emerging retail chains, had shown little interest in bottled soft drinks. They believed the broken glass and spillage created an image they didn't want for their large superstores. I remember when we visited Sam Walton in Bentonville, Arkansas. I was thirty years old and Mr. Walton, who was already growing the Walmart chain, was an imposing figure to a young marketing person like me. Nevertheless, we decided we had to persuade him on the merits of our new two-liter plastic bottle. I had rehearsed the following moment carefully. "Mr. Walton, here is our new unbreakable bottle for Pepsi and we think it's perfect for your superstores." As I said these words, I let the bottle drop from my hand to fall to the floor about three feet below. Everyone gasped, expecting to hear breaking glass. But the bottle bounced slightly and then started to roll across the floor. "What is that bottle made of?!" Mr. Walton asked. And I knew he was hooked.

This was the beginning of our most successful marketing campaign. It turned out that mass merchandisers and drug chains kept warehouse withdrawal sales data only on products in their stores. Since soft drinks were typically sold in these outlets, the chains did not know how large Pepsi and Coca-Cola sales could be. We knew that on a hot summer weekend, we could sell over a truckload of soft drinks through a single store.

At Pepsi, we had been working with McKinsey & Company on the early deployment of the Universal Product Code, later known as the bar code. Pepsi became the first consumer product to use the bar code as its way to track sales through chain stores. So now we could track Pepsi sales through Walmart. But we were still only one of 40,000 items sold through big chains, so we needed a way to get the attention of the chain's operating executives. Our idea was actually quite simple: We said to Walmart: "We are your new bank!" They were completely perplexed as to what we were talking about until we showed them in-store data that Pepsi turned over five times before they had to pay us. It didn't take more than a few seconds for them to comprehend the significance of that fact. It translated to millions of dollars of increased working capital for low-margin chains. We were really solving two big problems: No more broken glass on floors, enabling major new chains like Walmart to stock soft drinks, as we increased the cash flow of these retailers, our customers.

During my time as a management trainee at Pepsi, I had restocked many soft-drink supermarket shelves in the middle of the night and studied what I observed. I knew beverage display equipment was antiquated and it certainly wasn't intended for two-liter plastic bottles or the twelve-can packs that came later. Again using the theme, "Pepsi is your new bank," we designed a range of new merchandising equipment, including coolers and end-of-aisle displays. I had studied and worked briefly as an industrial designer at Donald Deskey Associates, one of the most famous design firms in the 1950s. So I jumped into helping design merchandise display equipment with much enthusiasm. Over the following three years, the average size of soft-drink shelf space more than tripled. Three years later, AC Nielsen gave Pepsi a special award for the longest consecutive market share increase of any brand it had ever measured. Three years after that, Pepsi became the largest-selling brand of the 40,000 stock-keeping units in large stores.

This experience illustrates the importance both of asking the right question and of thinking about marketing as an end-to-end system, not just an event. And, perhaps even more importantly, the importance of solving big customer problems.

A related story in plastic packaging was actually one I had nothing to do with. In the late 1970s, my brother David was head of marketing at H.J. Heinz and later CEO of H.J. Heinz USA. David and I always would do store checks. We both share the same sense of curiosity, and are always thinking that there has to be a better way. David was in a supermarket in Boston one day and discovered a barbeque sauce product, in a plastic bottle, being tested by Ocean Spray called "Squeeze 'n Season." He said, "Hmmm . . . Heinz ketchup is very difficult to pour from a glass bottle. What would happen if we offered it in a plastic bottle that you could squeeze, and made it easy for people to dispense? Would that solve a big problem?" Well, Ocean Spray's test product failed because the bottle then could not keep oxygen from permeating the plastic and spoiling the product. But after David's consumer research confirmed that Heinz ketchup in plastic solved a big consumer problem, he worked with American Can Company to develop a multilayered plastic package that really worked. It was one of the key success stories of Heinz's being able to go through an amazing era of growth while David was CEO.

Here are two powerful examples of how marketing innovation doesn't just have to be in the product itself, it can be in the package. It worked for Pepsi with the two-liter plastic beverage bottle, and it worked for Heinz with the squeezable plastic ketchup bottle. Adaptive innovators are always on the lookout for good ideas from other industries that they can adapt to their purpose.

Solving a major consumer problem is a great way to create a big business opportunity. However, this approach often requires a breakthrough in technology. Sometimes that can take years; and unless you have developed a proprietary process or patented approach, your competitive advantage may be short-lived. Nonetheless, being first-to-market is usually a big advantage and it is well worth going for.

Another industry with a wide range of big problems to solve is U.S. health care. Ours is the largest health care market in the world, at about $2.8 trillion, and it will continue to grow well into the future because of the aging of the American population, particularly the "Baby Boomers" who are starting to hit retirement.

One of the biggest problems for the industry and for its patients is the emergency room. Emergency rooms are frequently overcrowded, causing delays for patients that can turn into hours. Until recently, however, an emergency room was the only available place where you could see a doctor when you really needed one, like when you had a severe cut or needed a prescription. Getting in to see your primary care physician, if you even had one, could take days or weeks. Emergency rooms in hospitals were the only option for many patients—even for routine procedures. In response to this growing problem, the concept of urgent care centers began to arise about ten years ago. These retail units, staffed by a doctor and nurses, are usually in convenient retail locations and separate from hospitals. They are usually open at the highest traffic times, 9 a.m. until 9 p.m., seven days a week. The centers are typically very convenient for patients, with a doctor usually available to see a patient within just a few minutes at a cost that is a fraction of an emergency room visit. There are now over 9,000 urgent care centers in the U.S.! A recent health care research project I was involved with determined that fully twenty-four percent of American adults had been to an urgent care center an average of two times in the past year. That was a larger percentage of the population than owned iPads at the time of the research. Urgent care centers are solving a multibillion-dollar problem.

A related health care service that is solving a multibillion-dollar problem is one I am personally involved with. The industry is called telehealth and the company is MDLIVE. MDLIVE connects patients who want to talk with an experienced, licensed doctor right away about a nonemergency situation. Customers are connected by phone or secure Internet video twenty-four hours a day, seven days a week, even on weekends and holidays. If a prescription is appropriate, it can be sent instantly to your local pharmacy. MDLIVE is designed to give consumers convenient access to physicians. Talk about changing the rules in the typical patient experience of waiting days for an appointment and then another inconvenient wait at the doctor's office! The founder and CEO of this transformative company that is changing health care delivery is Randy Parker. I prize Randy as a friend as much as I value him as a business partner and admire his insight as an amazing visionary.

In scaling this business, Randy has had a really important insight: Low-acuity telehealth is growing rapidly, but it's vulnerable over time to margin compression. Randy is taking the end-to-end system he has created for low-acuity care and is expanding it into higher acuity and higher-margin health care services by specifically targeting very large, respected hospital systems. This should result in a network of geographic territories of health systems in every market across the country, focusing on access to specialists and second opinions. This story is a perfect example of an adaptive innovator using already gained domain expertise to take the business to an even better place.

The consumer era of health care will depend more and more on the network effect from the rapidly emerging world of digital health. People with domain knowledge are really helping to propel this exciting development in digital health. This includes highly respected voices like Scripps Institute's Dr. Eric Topol, NostaLabs' founder John Nosta, and Singularity University's Dr. Daniel Kraft. These three experts have helped me expand my own domain knowledge in this fast-growing field.

Using your industry domain expertise and thorough research to identify the really big problems to solve is a good place to start, as you begin the quest to create a billion-dollar business concept. But it is not the only approach.

3.

RELENTLESS PURSUIT OF "THERE HAS TO BE A BETTER WAY"

We cannot solve our problems with the same thinking we used when we created them.
                              —Albert Einstein

My whole life I have been driven by curiosity and wonder over the possibilities of new technologies. When I was a small boy, I didn't want toys. Instead, I loved getting my hands on electrical parts like lights, batteries, and switches. Later, I fell in love with electronics. I hung out with other kids like me and we would go down to Cortlandt Street in New York City, where surplus electronic radios, televisions, and thousands of used electronic parts were sold. When I was thirteen, I passed my ham radio license exam, and my call letters became K2HEP. When I was fourteen, I invented a fully electronic color television cathode ray tube and my dad helped me apply for a patent, but I was beaten out by a similar, competing patent from Ernest Orlando Lawrence, the cyclotron inventor, after whom Lawrence Livermore National Labs was named. Dr. Lawrence's invention was eventually sold to Sony and became the basis for the successful Trinitron television system.

During my teens, I built several experimental color

television sets, from spinning color wheels, to fully electronic projects with color filters, to a Heathkit color TV. I am not a trained engineer and I'm not a technical genius like Steve Wozniak, whose amazing gifts I described earlier. But I have an insatiable curiosity; and when I look at a business problem or a product, I constantly conclude, "There has to be a better way."

I guess that's why I so admire people who are driven to make new products much better than the current ones. Recently, I had the opportunity to spend some time with Wolfgang Puck at his award-winning restaurant, Spago, in Beverly Hills, California. He talked about his insatiable curiosity and his passion to continually make improvements in his culinary world. He said:

> When I opened the first Spago, I wanted it to be like a theater, so what did I do? I put the kitchen out into the dining room and they could see all the chefs cooking, the wood burning over a big charcoal grill and the tossing of the salad. Then guests used to come up to me and say, "So, Wolfgang, what do you have fresh today, what do you think I should eat tonight?" It was a completely different experience from the old style of restaurants where the waiters were dressed in tuxedos, and the chefs were somewhere in the back. Back then, nobody knew who the chefs were.
>
> Spago was really a first where actually the chef became the center point of the restaurant. Today, obviously, there are hundreds of chefs who own their own restaurant, but at that time there were maybe five in America who had really great restaurants.
>
> I always want to learn more, I'm always curious of what is going on. I still have to learn a lot of things, but I'm really curious about doing things and am always trying to do new things. If it's a sandwich shop at the airport or maybe a new style of soup for the supermarket, the opportunity to innovate always excites me.

The opportunity to innovate a promising new business always starts with a customer experience . . . usually one that is frustrating.

Getting a taxi in NYC can be incredibly frustrating, especially at shift changeover times. Limousine car services are expensive, and paying for wait time while one has a several-hour appointment makes it even more so. There's a billion-dollar problem waiting to be solved. Uber cofounders Travis Kalanick and Garrett Camp came up with a way to connect passengers needing rides with car service drivers needing passengers. It's a 10× better customer experience when compared to renting a traditional limo car service, a service that is incredibly simple to get when you want one; the price for a typical ride is usually much less expensive as well. Taking on the powerful big city taxi unions in urban markets like San Francisco and New York has not been easy, but Uber's success is already legendary. Founded in 2009, Uber's most recent valuation as a still-private company was $18 billion. Uber smartly uses exponential technologies and benefits from the network effect. Uber's founders have succeeded in creating a "better way" by solving a customer problem. Now they want to reinvent the entire industry of personalized transportation.

When I first heard about Airbnb, I was reminded of a car trip I had made with my parents through Pennsylvania when I was a boy, to visit the Amish country. In those days, it was before the Interstate Highway System and, as evening settled in one would look for *Vacancy* signs in front of people's homes along the roadway. These were called "bed-and-breakfast" lodgings and they provided many ordinary homeowners with a steady stream of income to open their home to travelers.

In 2008, Bryan Chesky, Joe Gebbia, and Nathan Blecharczyk cofounded Airbedandbreakfast.com, later shortened to Airbnb. They decided to build a comfortable lodging service at a disruptive price, using someone else's home or apartment. Technology has enabled a simple, easy customer experience. Today Airbnb provides access to accommodations in more than 34,000 cities in 190 countries, and has served over 15 million guests. Its market value is currently around $10 billion. This all came from an idea and then a passion to deliver overnight accommodations in a "better way."

I first met Michael Dell in 1990. The story of his entrepreneurial success was already folklore, about how Michael started his build-to-order PC company in his dorm room at the University of Texas. In the early 1990s, before Tim Berners-Lee had invented the web and before Jim Clark and Marc Andreessen had cofounded Netscape Communications as the first web browser company, everyone used fax machines. Intel and Microsoft had by then created an ecosystem through which many companies were buying and assembling PCs using standard parts to build pretty similar personal computers.

Michael Dell was convinced he could sell personal computers in a better way. What made his business model unique was this: If you faxed him or called him up, he would build you a customized personal computer fitted out exactly as you requested in terms of the processor, amount of memory, and size of the hard drive. He would also preload it with the software you chose. Because his overhead was low, so were his prices for a Dell computer. In those early days, Michael spent virtually no money on R&D and over time adopted a just-in-time supply-chain model with his vendors inventorying, at their expense, electronic components close to Dell's final assembly and test facility in Austin, Texas. Just at this time, Big Blue IBM was abandoning developing its own PC operating system to compete with Microsoft, and taking a huge write-off on IBM's version of a Windows-compatible operating system called OS2. Concurrently, Michael Dell's cheaper, faster, better, and more convenient business model was taking off.

Michael's path to success was not without some turbulent moments. By 1994, fax was no longer as relevant for customer ordering, as many of Dell's prospective buyers could request a built-to-order and disruptively priced Dell PC over the web. Michael nearly ran out of cash even as he scaled his supply chain with just-in-time final assembly. (He learned that leveraging his vendors' capital was a more complex proposition than one might expect.) Fortunately, Michael Dell reached out to two highly talented good friends of mine to mentor him through his "near-death" experience of cash pressures and to help realize important improvements in Dell's design and quality. Former Motorola EVP Mort Topfer became Dell's EVP of operations and was instrumental in helping Michael turn the company around when it got into trouble. Another longtime friend of mine, Mort Meyerson, had been one of Michael's earliest mentors. Mort is an excellent judge of people and known as a superb systems designer. He had been Ross Perot's partner and later CEO of the Perot-founded EDS. Michael Dell was fortunate to have such exceptional mentors.

More recently, Dell Computers has suffered with the decline of the personal computer. Michael has just taken his company private and seems as excited about the future as he was when he started the company. His insatiable curiosity and drive to find a better way is legendary. Michael is determined to lead the reinvention of Dell.

Uniqlo is a Japanese company that is now over thirty years old and was founded by Tadashi Yanai, today one of Japan's wealthiest entrepreneurs. Uniqlo has developed an extremely lightweight fabric that is perfect for an active, casual lifestyle. What's unique about Uniqlo clothing is its specially developed fabric that turns moisture evaporating from the body into heat by creating small air pockets. Most clothing lines are fashion brands known by their designer styles. Uniqlo built its success story around the uniqueness of the science of its fabrics. Its products are carefully engineered for practical considerations like warmth, wrinkle-resistance, and breathability. Uniqlo's "better way" is to offer very moderately priced clothing for young active customers who appreciate clothes that are quick drying, neutralize body odor, "breathe" while being worn, and are nearly light as air.

If you have ever been in a Uniqlo retail clothing store, you know it's a very different experience. Uniqlo has combined its disruptively priced business model aimed at a middle class seeking more affordable apparel with an exceptional retail customer experience. Uniqlo's lightweight clothes are trendy and the retail service and customer checkout queuing process is really impressive. Today, Uniqlo, with its flagship U.S. store on Fifth Avenue, is called one of the hottest retailers in New York City. They found a better way with a very unique solution.

Ted Turner and I had attended Brown University together in the early '60s. Ted later dropped out and became an entrepreneur. In 1977, he began broadcasting the games of his Atlanta Braves baseball team via satellite. Then he started thinking about delivering TV news in a "better way"—twenty-four hours a day. By 1980, he had created CNN and was broadcasting twenty-four-hour news across America from Atlanta. It was a radical idea at the time, and the incumbent network news broadcasters were highly skeptical that it could match the quality of their then thirty-minute nightly news shows. Ted Turner was taking advantage of new technologies that enabled CNN to disrupt the cost of news programming, and the big news networks at the time didn't fully appreciate what Ted was up to. When inexpensive consumer video cameras became popular, Ted Turner equipped nonunion freelance camera crews all over the world with video cameras so they could do live video reports via satellite back to Atlanta. Ted's "better way" to deliver news changed cable TV forever.

Another example of finding a better way for consumers is OpenTable. As the Internet was coming of age, OpenTable's founders believed there was a better way for customers to make reservations at restaurants. Using sophisticated scheduling platforms and great marketing, OpenTable has become the leader in a new field. It's a win for the customer because of the convenience, and it's a win for restaurant owners who can more easily fill their seats. OpenTable was recently acquired by Priceline, an early disruptor itself, for $2.6 billion.

A "BETTER WAY" IN BUSINESS-TO-BUSINESS

Knowledge work has been the driving force in business productivity for the past three decades. What began as tools to empower individuals later advanced to collaborative client/server systems for entire departments and even large functional business domains. Today they stretch across the entire value chain of how work gets done.

David Duffield and Aneel Bhusri lost their earlier company, PeopleSoft, in an unsolicited takeover by Oracle. Oracle wasn't that interested in PeopleSoft's technology as the client/server model was nearing the end of its technology growth cycle; what Oracle wanted was PeopleSoft's installed base of customers. Larry Ellison, the Oracle cofounder and CEO, understood customer-centric economics. He knew it was far less expensive to acquire companies like JD Edwards, Siebel Systems, and PeopleSoft to get their customers than to acquire customers organically. Larry also understood the importance of scale. He had no interest in PeopleSoft's technology, just the customers, whom he would convert to Oracle's broader family of enterprise solutions. It was a brilliant strategy for Oracle, but the acquisitions were not always friendly transactions.

Duffield and Bhusri realized they could take their human resources domain expertise and use it to build an even better company as a SaaS (Software-as-a-Service) company. "Workday" was born, and in just a few years it has gone from a dream in the cofounders' mind's eye to an excellent example of a better way to provide a B2B (business-to-business) service. Workday is a self-service, fully automated, in the cloud, simple to use set of tools for knowledge workers to collaborate in real time. Workday simplifies the work processes to organize, staff, and pay a global workforce.

Like Salesforce.com, Workday is an on-demand B2B

subscription service running in the cloud. Workday has ad-opted many of Apple's design principles by connecting the dots between many different domain expertise functions while retaining a very simplified user experience. One can think of Workday as combining payroll, HR management, performance management, time and attendance, and finan-cials. Workday makes it simple and uses the new exponen-tial technologies to create a very smart, very personalized end-to-end system. That's a better way of organizing work for businesses. Workday was founded in 2005, and today its market cap as a public company is approximately $16 billion.

Exponential growth in digital technologies is creating massive opportunities for new better-way companies. One I've enjoyed monitoring is Pure Storage. You may remember that, a few years ago, Apple stopped using spinning drives and moved to solid-state storage on its iMacs. It was an ex-pensive changeover because all-flash storage costs more, but it was the right thing to do, as solid-state storage was the future.

The same trend is happening in the enterprise space as new companies like Fusion-io, Violin Memory, and Pure Storage have stepped in to compete with established firms like IBM. Pure Storage moved quickly with a better way of delivering a storage array with hundreds of terabytes of solid-state storage that was plug-compatible, all for less than the cost of spinning disks. Pure Storage's better way wasn't just a less-expensive product. It was a complete end-to-end system that could fit into data centers. It was an important better way for large enterprises making big com-mitments to the cloud.

If technology is the domain of a new business, the chal-lenge for adaptive innovators in pursuing a better way is to scale its size and to lock in an installed base of custom-ers before a new technology commoditizes. New compa-nies with very talented people who are already up to speed with important domain expertise enjoy a powerful advan-tage. Technology is game changing, but at the same time, technology is commoditizing at an unprecedented rate. For today's entrepreneur, your sustainable value will be an unrivaled customer experience, commanding domain expertise, your network effect, and how adaptive and innovative your business is in getting work done fast and frugally. It's just that simple . . . and it's just that hard.

In the end, the relentless pursuit of "there has to be a better way" can lead to huge, exciting, transformative businesses. Perpetually embracing the standard of making things better is the sort of moving-target attitude that will keep a business perpetually dynamic and viable.

The drive to find a "better way" to improve products and services has been going on for ages, and it remains a superb mindset to underpin new business success. Finding a better way usually starts with curiosity and then develops into a relentless passion. Converting a potential business concept to a truly transformative business, however, often requires more. That's why the possibility of "disruptive pricing," discussed in the next chapter, and enabled by the new exponential technologies, offers such a decisive advantage in building a billion-dollar concept.

4.

DISRUPTIVE PRICING:
THERE'S NO PLACE TO HIDE

Your margin is my opportunity.
　　—Jeff Bezos,
　　　　founder and CEO, Amazon

Before 1990, Walmart didn't have a single store in Pennsylvania or California. Founded in 1962, today Walmart is in both of those places and more. It's one of the world's largest public corporations and the largest retailer. Its income surpasses the GDP of many countries. Walmart has a huge number of people at minimum-wage compensation working in their retail stores, and their workforce worldwide is about 2 million people, about 1.4 million in the U.S. Walmart became the largest purchaser in the world of products mostly sourced from China, and was a major factor in establishing China as the world's factory, just as India had become the world's back office.

Sam Walton was one of those rare innovators who changed the rules for an entire industry. He started out in rural communities and built the largest, most successful retail firm in the world, eventually coming to the big cities last. He focused on customers who were basically rural and lower-income people. They needed and wanted the same product that higher-income people wanted, but at much lower prices. Sam Walton's mass merchandising model answered that need, through its focus on disruptive pricing.

Walmart, with sales of nearly half a trillion dollars, may also be in danger of being disrupted—not immediately, but over time. Why? Walmart's online sales were a mere $9 billion last year. As *Wired* wrote in early 2013: "Walmart undoubtedly looks at that $9 billion and sees nowhere to go but up. The other figure they're looking at is $61 billion: Amazon's net sales for its most recent fiscal year." And well they should, because Amazon's sales jolted up to $75 billion by the end of 2013.

THE BATTERING RAM OF DISRUPTIVE PRICING

Walmart targeted a blue-collar, rural, lower-middle-class shopper, many of whom had aspirations of living a traditional middle-class lifestyle. Amazon is aimed at the new adaptive middle class, short on both cash and time, but willing to shop in new ways to attain value. Amazon's model has no retail stores, but it hires those same low-wage people Walmart does, except they operate supply centers for same-day delivery. Amazon's people all interface with the customer through technology, whereas Walmart's team has interacted with the customer as greeters at the door and people who interrupted their shelf-stocking to guide you to products in the store.

Wired calls Amazon "Jeff Bezos' battering ram." For Walmart, a battering ram at the gates is exactly what it may be. Amazon is building the model for the exceptional customer experience of the future. What Jeff Bezos has done brilliantly is create a customer experience driven by predictive, Big Data analytics, running on massively powerful cloud computing systems to project the products and services you want, based on tracking your shopping behavior. As the store for everything, Amazon is building supply centers all around the country to anything you wanted the same day—any product or service you picked. They're even getting into fresh food! Orchestrated by powerful cloud computers, Amazon permits only the supply chain between it and your home or—with services like Kindle, to your mobile devices. Intermediary processes, which traditionally were done by knowledge workers in an earlier era of information management, are now automated. Work that was supervised by people in high-skilled middle-management jobs getting paid a lot of money has become computerized and intermediated. Heeding the Amazon model, corporations are being hollowed out—one after another—and middle managers are being replaced by automation, smart robots, and predictive analytics. The call centers and order-takers they supervised have all vanished.

The power of Amazon's concept is centered on disruptive pricing. It has already shaken up the book publishing world and is serving notice to virtually every brick-and-mortar retailer. But in the end, it's all about customer satisfaction, and Jeff Bezos is brilliantly coupling disruptive prices with exceptional customer convenience. His product selection can be much broader than that of any other brick-and-mortar retailer, including Walmart. He provides real-time customer reviews of products, and he is delivering the goods to Amazon's customers ever faster.

Here's what is really interesting when one compares Amazon to Walmart. Both have lots of workers. But Amazon has achieved exceptional customer experience by taking advantage of the most advanced data science and automated intelligent systems. Customers love shopping at Amazon; Amazon works hard to make its customers very smart, and it also prospects these happy customers with attractive offers personalized for each individual. Where are most of Amazon's employees positioned? Either in technology or in the supply chain. Amazon is building large same-day-delivery supply centers across the U.S. and is aggressively hiring supply-center workers. But Amazon is also using robots in these supply centers. In fact, in 2012, Amazon paid $775 million to acquire the robot company Kiva Systems. Amazon doesn't need nearly as many mid- and higher-skilled workers across layers of management to implement process as Walmart does, because Bezos uses the most sophisticated technology whenever he can. Amazon is growing, but it is also substituting capital for labor when it thinks its smart systems offer an edge. Amazon is adding jobs, but it's staffing with entirely different skills than its big retailer competitors. My summary of the Amazon formula in a nutshell:

Exceptional customer experience + there has to be a better way + lowest prices = adaptive innovation at its best.

Disruptive pricing has never been more possible than it is today. Using cloud services and unstructured data analytics, these technologies are becoming more and more affordable tools to enhance the customer experience and to do so at lower-than-expected prices. That's a great combination that can create billion-dollar opportunities in industry after industry.

Another example of disruptive pricing is a company I mentioned earlier in the emerging telehealth space, MDLIVE. MDLIVE gives patients immediate access to board-certified doctors and therapists on their phone or via Internet video 24/7.

Several years ago, its founder and CEO, Randy Parker, who, as I mentioned, is a business partner with me, recognized that the traditional medical model that has sustained itself for decades is rapidly breaking down for a number of reasons:

- It's expensive to visit the doctor.
- It can take days or weeks to get an appointment.
- The doctor is too rushed/busy.
- Your doctor generally won't talk with you on the phone to answer a question because in many cases it's an inefficient use of the doctor's time.
- The Internet has become a huge source of instant medical info that did not exist in the past, and this changes the doctor/patient relationship in some cases.

Randy Parker has built a cutting-edge, end-to-end system built around the customer that can deliver a more convenient, superior patient experience using telehealth, at a fraction of the cost of an in-person visit. It costs about $40 for a convenient telehealth consultation with an experienced, licensed doctor, compared to around $125 for an in-person consultation. Today, the service encompasses low-acuity conditions like bronchitis or urinary tract infections; but in the future, MDLIVE intends to provide convenient access to specialists. Disruptive pricing is a key component of Randy's formula. As more and more Americans are forced into high-deductible plans, they will pay for many routine medical costs completely out of their own pocket, and will become far more aware of how expensive medical costs actually are. For this very impactful reason, companies like MDLIVE are likely to play a significant role. Earlier, I said Randy Parker's next phase is to move beyond low-acuity telehealth to enter higher value and more complex health services. Adaptive innovators don't have time to pause and enjoy their success.

Here's another example of a company that's succeeding with the use of disruptive pricing. It's called Warby Parker, and the primary problem it's addressing is the high cost of eyeglasses. The concept was started in 2012 by a Wharton Business School student, Neil Blumenthal, and three classmates, Andrew Hunt, Jeffrey Raider, and David Gilboa. They decided to go up against industry giant Luxottica—owner of LensCrafters, Pearle Vision and Sunglass Hut—according to an article in the *Wharton Digital Press*. With an average industry price for glasses around $250, Warby Parker glasses sell, primarily online, for only $95. Not only that, the company has other unique features:

- The designs offered are hip and stylish.
- They offer an at-home trial program (test five at a time for free).
- They give a free pair of glasses for someone in need for every pair they sell at regular price.

The concept is powerful because it's built around a disruptive price, but it has additional appeal to younger consumers, particularly Millennials. The company has attracted major funding from sophisticated investors and is rapidly expanding. And, according to the same article, the global market for eyeglasses is projected at $96 billion by 2015. The potential here is mindboggling.

Closer to home, here's another disruptive pricing example that recently attracted the attention of my brother David and me. It's a company in the shaving category called 800razors.com. The founders, Phil Masiello and Steven Krane, approached us because of our experience with consumer marketing, particularly direct-response television.

800razors.com sells high-quality three- and five-blade men's and women's razors exclusively over the Internet. Phil and Steven's research showed that there is a lot of customer dissatisfaction with the price of branded high-quality razors. In fact, the price is so high that many stores put razors on locked shelves to prevent pilfering. Having to track down a busy store manager to unlock the razor shelf adds to the frustration of would-be buyers. Phil and Steven created a low-cost fulfillment system that can deliver 800razors.com shaving products with quality comparable to that of the big razor brands, at about half their cost. 800razors.com also has a powerful customer information system using the cloud and data analytics to help provide a low-cost, high-quality customer experience. We believe these two adaptive innovators have a model with a decent chance of disrupting the traditional razor category. To achieve real price disruption, it's not about making modifications to an existing supply chain. It's about reinventing the chain from start to finish.

In 2013, I got involved in the possible acquisition of a once pioneering smartphone business, BlackBerry, after its board started a process to sell the company. In 2012, Shane Maine, Gord McMillan, and I were cofounding partners of the acquisition and credit finance company Inflexionpoint.

We had lined up over $4 billion of potential financing to acquire BlackBerry, but BlackBerry's board members later changed their minds and ended the process to sell the company. Instead, they decided to hire John Chen, one of the most respected high-tech turnaround executives, to become CEO. We had estimated that about 6,500 employees were assigned to the device side of BlackBerry. As Inflexionpoint Asia was already in the components supply chain and IT distribution business, we were very familiar with the cost model throughout the supply chain needed to build a high-quality smartphone and sell it in emerging markets. Our estimates were that we could run a device line of business with fewer than 500 people; we wouldn't need 6,500 people.

John Chen understood that the device business had to be run on a much lower-cost business model, so one of his first decisions was to outsource the design and contract manufacturing of all BlackBerry devices to Foxconn, the same contract resource that manufactures the iPhone for Apple. At the same time as we were pursuing BlackBerry, Microsoft was in the process of acquiring Nokia's mobile phone line of business, which employed 32,000 people and was losing hundreds of millions of dollars a quarter. Can Microsoft completely reinvent the Nokia supply chain to compete with mobile companies focused on disruptive pricing? One indication of the direction Microsoft is taking is that, in mid-July 2014, it announced it was laying off 18,000 workers, most from the Nokia acquisition, its largest layoff ever, and apparently part of its attempt to become more nimble.

Although we ultimately did not acquire BlackBerry, we had considerable domain expertise in the mobile-device value chain with our Inflexionpoint Asia CEO, Neeraj Chauhan. We were confident that we could market a very high-quality mobile product, with excellent customer satisfaction at less than half the price of the international brands. As I mentioned earlier, that's why we launched Obi - Connect Smarter devices in Delhi, India, in 2014 at a disruptive price of about USD $200. We are optimistic about carving out a meaningful market share in this booming category.

So, what might aspiring entrepreneurs take away from these examples? **The previous era of business opportunity was about lifting out functions and turning them over to a lower-cost supplier. The new era requires completely redesigning the entire premise of one's business to improve the customer experience.** The belief that "There has to be a better way" requires thoughtfully redesigning an end-to-end system, always beginning with the assumption that customers are getting really smart. In parallel, costs must be systemically reduced. The priority shifts away from lowering the cost of current processes to empowering adaptive innovators in key positions inside the company and asking them to come up with radical new ways to serve customers much better and cheaper. A total rethinking of the business model and its supporting business process is necessary to enable the economics of disruptive pricing to work for your organization.

Disruptive pricing is a powerful business concept. By itself alone, it has the potential to create a successful business. But combine it with a lights-out customer experience never seen before, and you have the potential for a truly transformative business concept, as you will see in the next chapter.

5.

DELIVER A LIGHTS-OUT CUSTOMER EXPERIENCE

If you're competitor-focused, you have to wait until there is a competitor doing something. Being customer-focused allows you to be more pioneering.
—Jeff Bezos,
founder and CEO, Amazon

In 2006, when Julia Hartz and her husband Kevin founded Eventbrite, they weren't just interested in selling tickets to major events across the globe. They wanted to give people access to all kinds of events—large and small—more easily than ever before. They also wanted to expose people to the events most suited to their interests through the power of social connections.

One such event, the Tough Mudder—a grueling ten- to twelve-mile military-style obstacle course—exemplifies the power of the Eventbrite platform. By helping people discover the events their social connections are signing up for, Eventbrite elevates the visibility of activities like the Tough Mudder, increasing enrollment and engagement. Today, the Eventbrite platform showcases many thousands of events in cities around the world, generating about a billion dollars of event sales annually. Julia and Kevin's success has been driven by their single-minded focus on the customer experience.

Of all the elements essential to a billion-dollar business concept, none is more important than creating a lights-out customer experience. Consider the brands that most impress us for the stellar customer experiences they create. Among them are certainly:

- Amazon
- Apple and Apple Stores
- Google
- Four Seasons Hotels and Resorts
- Starbucks
- Virgin Group companies
- BMW

Except for Four Seasons and BMW, all these companies are relatively new or were known only to a select clientele twenty years ago. A couple—like Amazon and Google—didn't even exist more than two decades ago. It's very hard to achieve and sustain star status—to acquire and preserve Wow! status—in providing an exceptional customer experience.

Scroll through Amazon's book department, and you'll find more than twenty book titles dedicated to "The Wow Factor" and how to get it. Tom Peters has even written a book titled *The Pursuit of Wow!* Achieving a Wow! response may be difficult, but the hardest part is re-creating Wow! consistently, achieving an extraordinary result again and again, especially when conditions are less than ideal. And once the result becomes routine and predictably reliable, yesterday's "Wow!" usually shrivels up into today's "So what?"

Lights-out customer experiences are almost always achieved by leaders who raise the bar, not companies playing catch-up. Today, we're saturated with products that have become commoditized. Less and less differentiation exists between products, and new products are coming out all the time. It's often harder to pinpoint a brand and say what separates that brand from something else. A few people have done that really well. BMW is one, because it says, "we're the ultimate driving machine," and whenever you think of BMW you connect with its driving experience. When Apple sells its product, it always talks about the experience of the product.

Products that tell their stories, that build a reputation of being highly personal, and that make YOU feel special as their customer are likeliest to succeed. There are also brands that are very broad-based. You don't associate them with a particular product, but they are seamlessly and effortlessly in the background. Amazon, the store for everything, is a service like that. Amazon could basically sell anything under its retail umbrella. Virgin has similar brand breadth. Virgin Group has put their name on a railroad. They've put it on a cola-drink. They've put it on a mobile phone. They've put it on an airline. They've put it on music. How can they make a brand work across so many categories? It doesn't always work, but when it does, it's because there are a certain set of attributes or expectations that people have of anything Virgin does. I hadn't flown on Virgin America Airlines before a few years ago, but I had an expectation that it would be a great experience. And guess what? It lived up to the great experience I had expected. That's because Virgin always goes out of its way to make its experience something special. Richard Branson's Virgin Group has excelled in making experiences special, no matter what the product. Virgin understands that building a customer relationship is the heart of a successful business. **The goal is to engage customers in an experience journey: Getting customers to buy the product or service is only the *beginning* of a relationship. The transaction is not the destination, but the launching point of a long journey.**

In January 2011, Richard Branson penned a memorable blog on customer service in which he said: "[d]elivering good customer service requires frontline workers to receive support from co-workers—in effect, a chain reaction of teamwork that is consistent from beginning to end.

And the chain of assistance is only as strong as its weakest link.... No company can train its front-end people to handle every situation, but you can strive to create an environment in which they feel at ease 'doing as they would be done by.'" Personal service 24/7—pivotal to the success of so many businesses—is a matter of training and judgment, he said, and, it must start "at the top. If your senior people don't get it, even the strongest links further down the line can become compromised."

Richard Branson is dedicated to broad-range opportunism, and he's not the sort to bet the farm on just a single strategy. "Opportunities are like buses," he says with admirably cool confidence, "there's always another one coming." What drives Branson is that he perpetually plays his cards from a solidly built hand—unexpectedly disrupting a host of industries "on the customer's behalf."

And yet, how many firms don't comprehend the simple service standard that Virgin businesses embrace? Think of the experience of shopping at old-line stores like Sears or Kmart, where it is so difficult to find someone to help you find the product you want. Or about almost any government service like the Post Office or the ordeal of trying to get your driver's license renewed. You end up waiting in frustrating lines and dealing with workers who clearly couldn't care less about you, the customer. Many online companies today make it nearly impossible for you to contact them—no email address, no phone number, no contact information. All they have are FAQs, which are helpful only some of the time. What are they thinking? For sure, it's not customer service. For many, it's customer *disservice*.

Flying on most airlines has become almost as frustrating as dealing with the government, but we are beginning to see some changes that recognize the importance of the customer experience. Delta's new terminals at LaGuardia Airport in New York, for example, have plenty of comfortable seats with iPads, WiFi, and outlets that allow you to connect to the Internet while you order a beverage or a meal without leaving your seat. Delta didn't dream up this service idea by studying the competition. They got there by studying the customer. Customers aren't passively acquired. If you want them to remember you with profound regard, then you must go out and study their needs and desires with intensity.

A generalization I learned years ago still applies across every industry I have worked in. It typically costs between five to eight times more to replace the sales revenue from a lost customer than if you had not lost that customer in the first place. Even more importantly, it typically costs between ten and fifteen times more to replace the lost profits from a lost customer than if you hadn't lost that customer in the first place. This is not an exact science rule, but it's very indicative of why a customer plan and customer metrics are so important. Among the most important customer metrics for the largest wireless carriers are customer churn rates.

A great example of how important holding on to your customers is illustrated at MetroPCS, a prepaid, regional wireless carrier that I was involved in from its start. CEO Roger Linquist had lots of domain expertise in the wireless industry before he founded his disruptive price carrier. The company has been a huge success, first going public on the NYSE and later being acquired by T-Mobile. Roger came up with a very low cost of customer acquisition using an offer where the customer buys the phone, but doesn't have to sign a two-year contract, as was normal with the much larger wireless carriers like Verizon and AT&T. By not requiring that contract, Roger was able to shape his offer to especially appeal to the most price-sensitive consumers. But for the business model to work, he had to keep his monthly customer churn low. Roger achieved low churn by keeping his prices way under the major carriers, and by building a reputation for an excellent customer experience. It worked beautifully.

EXCEPTIONAL CUSTOMER EXPERIENCE
AT THE CENTER

No doubt about it, those companies that make it their mission to deliver a light's-out customer experience are those with the best chance of transforming their industries. Think of what Howard Schultz has created with Starbucks. He completely reinvented the coffee shop. His passion to deliver a welcoming, efficient environment with exceptional products is indeed inspired and groundbreaking. Starbucks' employees are beautifully trained to give professional but friendly service in an environment that is alive and fun to be part of. Even though he charges a premium price, customers are happy to pay it because of the incredible experience they receive. His whole culture is built around the customer. That is his secret, and it is a great lesson for any entrepreneur.

Apple has been a frontrunner in optimizing the customer experience: in design innovation, in visioning the computer as a media/communications tool light-years beyond a mere number-crunching machine, and in personalizing the technology buying experience as well as the incredible service at the Genius Bar in Apple retail stores. Apple has also been a pioneer in drawing customers into the product-design experience as partners. Apple took the revolutionary approach of allowing external developers to build apps for its App Store—a model that has been instrumental in Apple's gaining market leadership, and one that so many platform vendors are now emulating in order to keep up. By leaning on external players, enterprises in today's fast-moving market can quickly deliver products and services that customers might not have ever imagined before.

When it came out with the iPhone, Apple didn't just say, "Gee, it can run on 3G and that's different than 2G, so now you can do photos on the iPhone." Apple said, "We have something in our end-to-end system for 3G called App Stores." Now well over a billion apps have been downloaded that take advantage of 3G. Apple also provided some very simple tools for developers to be able to grab objects, modify them, and put them together. Pretty easily and at very low expense, independent innovators could create unique apps that could sit on top of an iPhone 3. The app-creating experience has helped to mold an entire legion of innovation-trained entrepreneurial talent, from whom I'm sure many future business innovators will be drawn. Getting approved as a certified App Store developer is no easy experience. Apple is relentless, insisting that developers meet its very high standard with no compromises in the customer experience.

While I'm a proponent of disruptive pricing, some companies have been so successful with exceptional customer experience that they can go with a premium price strategy and still be very successful. Apple is the obvious best example. At its Worldwide Developers Conference in June 2014, Apple raised the bar on an even better customer experience for Apple users who have several different Apple products like iPhone, iPad, and MacBook Air. Now these products will be even better integrated so users can easily go from device to device within the Apple ecosystem without losing a beat. In late 2014, Apple is expected to introduce its next generation iPhone 6 and its new iOS 8 software, again raising the bar. This includes sapphire glass, much larger and higher-resolution displays, larger screen, thinner designs, and longer battery life. These are incremental improvements, but important to Apple users who expect the most for the premium prices Apple charges.

In 2013, a *Wall Street Journal* headline declared: "Apps Rocket Toward $25 Billion in Sales." The article said: "Nearly five years after Apple kicked off the mobile-apps craze, the industry is booming. App stores run by Apple and Google Inc. now offer more than 700,000 apps each. With so many apps to choose from, consumers are estimated to spend on average about two hours a day with apps." **The app has become a freshly laid cornerstone in business development. Apps have become the kernels of fledgling business ventures, involving huge numbers of new entrepreneurs.**

"Some app companies are scrambling for new revenue streams and expanding beyond the current leading money pots: ads and in-app purchases," the *Journal* article added.

Dennis Ratner is a hair cutting and hair styling chain entrepreneur, and a good friend, who has achieved tremendous business success. Ratner Companies started with one salon and two stylists back in 1974. Led by Ratner and his cofounder and former wife, Ann Ratner, it is today the largest privately owned and operated chain of hair salons in the U.S. It employs 12,000 associates in its 900 salons in sixteen states across the nation. They launched their first Hair Cuttery with start-up capital of just $5,000 and sketched out their strategic plan on a cocktail napkin during dinner. We were chatting recently, and Dennis told me that he didn't go to college but took a training course to become a hair stylist. His voice was charged with excitement as he talked of his passion to create the best place in the world for his employees to work. He is relentless about training his employees on the skills needed to deliver an exceptional customer experience. He vividly describes how he has built a culture of accountability through Ratner Group, and his employees and loyal clients love it!

Has there been a material payoff for their dedicated business commitment? Dennis enjoys homes in Virginia; Aspen, Colorado; and Palm Beach, Florida; and he has a personal jet to travel between them. But it's not his wealth that excites him. Dennis' fulfillment comes even more from building something important to his customers, and from the satisfaction of being the best at what he does.

As I have said many times, success often hinges on asking the right questions. Nowhere is that truer than in creating an exceptional customer experience. Not only do you need to ask penetrating questions when you launch a business; you have to keep asking them as your business evolves. And you must vigilantly ask tough and demanding questions when you do anything that might alter or disrupt either the reality or the perception of the customer's experience. Pay more attention to serving today's customer-in-control, not to short-sighted, petty ways to squeeze pennies out of the till.

As Zappos CEO and LinkExchange cofounder Tony Hsieh has said, "Chase the vision, not the money; the money will end up following you."

You might be surprised to learn that after I had joined Apple, and in all of the many times I was with Steve Jobs and Bill Gates, we never talked about how much money any of us would make. In those early days, the conversations were always about ideas, products, and how we needed to work together. There were the predictable arguments between Steve and Bill. Steve was always focused on user-experience design, and Bill—always the pragmatic adaptive innovator—focused on how Microsoft's software apps could help scale the Mac. These conversations took place decades ago, but my memories remain fresh. I have never to this day met two people more focused than Steve Jobs and Bill Gates. Both brilliant, both articulate, both determined they were right, both persuasive, and both always standing their ground. Bill would rock back and forth in his chair as conversations became more intense, while Steve would pace the room constantly, using his hands to gesture and make a point. Bill wanted Steve to license the Mac operating system; Steve was adamant that Apple would never do this, as he insisted he didn't want any compromises in the quality of the experience. Steve constantly accused Bill of stealing his ideas, and Bill kept reminding Steve that these weren't Apple's ideas and that Steve had in fact taken Xerox PARC's ideas and adapted them. Steve *had* to have Microsoft's Multiplan spreadsheet app (this was years before Microsoft Office), and Bill knew Steve Jobs was the best systemic designer in the world to adapt PARC's high-cost inventions to an affordable nontechnical user system. Silicon Valley is different today. Bankers are now power players, and for them, it's all about the money. But in those early days, it was *never* about the money. It's refreshing to still see some of the most successful young entrepreneur geniuses still inspired by noble causes and putting customers first.

Another great example of a company totally focused on the customer experience is The RealReal, an online luxury products company founded by serial entrepreneur Julie Wainwright. She created this company after the economic shock of 2008 to deliver luxury women's fashion products and accessories at an affordable price. She does this by attracting "providers," who may have used an item, like a designer handbag, only once or twice. The availability of these goods is listed online with The RealReal, on consignment, for someone else to acquire. Julie's team makes sure the products are in excellent condition, and are packaged beautifully, and deliver them with wonderful, personal customer attention. All of her daily business metrics are focused on measuring her customer's experience, and she has built the entire company's culture around the customer. In just three years in business, Julie is now on track to do over $100 million in revenue. And she is expanding into men's fashions and the huge jewelry category.

Wolfgang Puck has built a global culinary empire, including upscale fine dining restaurants, Wolfgang Puck Expresses—which sell gourmet pizzas in airports and universities—and huge catering events, like one following the Academy Awards. In an industry known for high employee turnover, I asked Wolfgang why so many of his employees have stayed with him for years and years. He said, "We're not in the food service business. We're in the hospitality business. It's all about giving the customer an unforgettable experience." He went on to say that hiring the right people, training them well to treat customers like family, while delivering delicious food using the best ingredients, is the way to delight the customer. Wolfgang personally goes to the fish market early in the morning to pick out the best seafood. And he sources vegetables from Chino Farms in Southern California because they taste like they came out of his mother's garden when he was growing up in Austria. If you ever have the opportunity to visit Wolfgang's flagship restaurant, Spago, in Beverly Hills, Wolfgang will be there on most nights. He makes it a point to stop by every table in the restaurant to chat with customers, let them take photographs and, importantly, make them feel totally welcome. Wolfgang's success is based on treating his customers like friends invited to his home. He really gets it.

Speaking of restaurants, in Florida, I'm chairman of the South Florida PDQ restaurant franchise, started by my close friend Outback Steakhouse cofounder Tim Gannon. The parent company, PDQ restaurants, was founded in Tampa, Florida, by another Outback Steakhouse cofounder, Bob Basham. This is a booming business in the "fast-casual" category, with an average meal ticket price of $7.50. PDQ serves only chicken and salads, no beef. The menu items are few and the ingredients always the best and fresh every day. In fact, Tim points out that he doesn't have a freezer in any PDQ restaurant, because he insists that no food should be saved for the next day. Cofounder and CEO Tim Gannon makes sure that leftover food always goes to a nonprofit organization that aids hungry people needing help. Tim is an expert at flavorings. (He invented one of the most successful food phenomena ever, the "Bloomin' Onion" at Outback.) Food always tastes good at a PDQ, and its reputation has spread fast through each community. What makes PDQ such a superb customer experience is its use of a simple repeatable system augmented with technology support and excellent training of the personnel.

Electronic displays flash green and yellow time scores for every order. Green means they are on track to deliver your order in two minutes. Yellow means it's running closer to three minutes. PDQ is rigorous with its customer-experience systems and its employee training. When it's raining, an employee even walks each customer to the car with an umbrella! The flashing time reports are at the cutting edge of the modern customer's technological awareness, but the umbrella is a vestige of old-time service. Tim

Gannon has lunch at one of his PDQ restaurants every day. He is a super-nice person and loves talking with his customers. His employees know Tim really cares about every detail, and they work hard to please customers and to please Tim. I love having lunch there too. Everybody is always smiling, including customers and workers, no matter how busy the restaurants are. The system of getting people through the ordering process and getting them to a freshly cleaned table just seems to happen automatically. But I know how careful Tim is to sweat every detail. Each system is simplified as much as possible. It feels spontaneous; but, like a Steve Jobs product introduction, it's a series of operating practices that are rehearsed as carefully as a theater performance. **The point: Businesses can and should couple the modern and the traditional when it makes sense to deliver a positive, memorable, and re-creatable customer experience.**

How about this observation from a July 2014 article in *USA Today*? "McDonald's makes the worst burgers. KFC offers the worst chicken. . . . This according to 32,405 *Consumer Reports* subscribers, in a survey whose results are bound to leave some high-powered fast-food executives scratching their heads today." What are the executives of these companies thinking? How can they let smaller chains deliver much better-tasting recipes?

When I talk about disrupting industries by delivering a lights-out customer experience, it's not just technology or social media companies. It can happen even in a huge, traditional industry like restaurants. Chipotle, for example, which offers healthy, delicious foods, is an innovative, rapidly growing chain with a very high P/E or price earnings ratio of around 56. That's even higher than Google, which stands at about 30. McDonald's, by contrast, has a P/E of only 18. McDonald's, by the way, invested heavily in Chipotle in the 1990s, but pulled out in 2006 to focus on its (not very highly rated) core hamburger brand.

THE POWER OF EXPERIENCE MARKETING

In the 1970s, Pepsi was largely a regional success story: We were successful in a few Midwest states, but we weren't very successful in the high-growth Southwestern region. In fact, in markets like San Antonio, Texas, we were outsold nine-to-one by Coca-Cola. People in that market had never even thought about *trying* a different soft drink. They were completely satisfied with Coke. It was a great brand and it tasted good. Why would they want to switch to another product like Pepsi? The Pepsi Challenge was a campaign designed to capture the expression of longtime Coke drinkers who had never even thought about having a Pepsi in their entire life—the *Ah-hah!* moment when they experienced Pepsi and found *unexpected satisfaction.*

The marketing challenge: To document that ten- to fifteen-second surprise when they discover, in a blind taste test, that they actually prefer Pepsi over Coca-Cola. I worked with Harry Hersh and his team to create the Pepsi Challenge as a way for people to taste-test the difference. This was a true test and it was filmed in a way that made it seem like it wasn't staged, because it wasn't. One of the commercials was particularly successful: It was of a grandmother from San Antonio, Texas, with her little granddaughter sitting right behind her, looking over her shoulders as the grandmother took the Pepsi Challenge taste test. The grandmother said, "I don't know why I'm taking this test. I've never had a Pepsi in my life. I've always had Coca-Cola, so why am I even doing this?" The granddaughter says nothing. The camera cuts to her as she watches her grandmother with great interest.

The grandmother takes a taste from one of the unidentified cups, and then she takes a taste from the other unidentified cup. Then she is asked to choose one, and she makes her pick. Then the person administering the test asks, "Would you like to know what you picked?" The grandmother says, "Well, yes." When she learns she picked Pepsi, the grandmother says, "I can't believe it." The little granddaughter, says, "Grandma, you picked Pepsi." The grandmother says, "I've never had a Pepsi in my life. *I can't believe* I picked Pepsi over Coke."

Consider that fifteen-second exchange, with the granddaughter's expression as she watches her grandmother taste both colas and her grandmother's surprise upon discovering that she picked Pepsi. That was the outcome we were looking for in the Pepsi Challenge. This skirmish really started the cola wars between Pepsi and Coke. Here we were, a product being trounced by the market leader. Coke was then considered the most valuable trademark in the world, and we were taking them on and saying, no, we will let the customer decide which product they think is best, purely on the taste.

That shows you how powerful customer opinions are. It also shows you how we uncovered a multibillion-dollar opportunity. In time, in that original San Antonio market where we were trailing badly to Coke, we actually passed them. Then Harry Hersh and Jack Pingel took the Pepsi Challenge to the whole state of Texas, and eventually across the United States. We became the leading selling soft-drink brand in U.S. supermarkets. Some years later, Nielsen named us the largest-selling consumer packaged good in America. A lot of the credit goes to the power of the experience marketing that we started with the Pepsi Challenge campaign in San Antonio.

The Pepsi Challenge caught the attention of Steve Jobs at Apple, where he had created a computer for nontechnical people. He wanted to sell this amazing new experience. This is the main reason I was hired at Apple; to bring experience marketing to Apple. This was before consumer advertising had arrived in Silicon Valley. We used these experience marketing principles to develop the famous "1984" commercial that successfully launched the first Mac computer. Leveraging a lights-out customer experience with compelling, experience marketing is an incredibly powerful combination.

MEASURING THE CUSTOMER EXPERIENCE

More and more savvy marketing authorities share my own conviction: The best way to measure and track customer experience is by using the Net Promoter Score, a metric developed by Fred Reichheld, Bain & Company, and Satmetrix Consulting.

The Net Promoter Score, or NPS, is based on a simple, single query called "The Ultimate Question" asked of people who have tried the product. The question is: On a scale of 0 to 10 (0 being worst and 10 being best), "How likely would you be to recommend this product (or service) to a friend or relative?"

Those who give a 9 or 10 rating absolutely love the product and are considered "promoters," while those that rate it 0 to 6 dislike the product and are considered "detractors." The ones in the middle, who rate it 7 or 8, really don't have a strong opinion and are indifferent. The actual calculation of the Net Promoter Score is done by simply subtracting the percentage of "detractors" from the percentage of "promoters."

NPS scores vary widely among companies, and can range, in theory, from –100 percent to 100 percent. In fact, a very few companies have NPS scores of 50 percent or higher, which are considered very high. Successful companies like Apple, Amazon, Costco, and Google would fall in this select group. These high NPS scores mean customers are validating their exceptional customer experiences. By contrast, a number of companies or services that deliver poor customer service can have NPS scores of –20 percent or worse. It is unlikely these companies will remain in business over the long run unless they significantly improve their scores.

Think to yourself of a terrific restaurant you have just discovered or a movie you absolutely loved. You are likely to call your best friend and share the good news. You, in effect, are a "promoter." Likewise, if you just ate in a new restaurant and hated it, you are just as likely to make a call to a friend and warn against it. In that way, you are a "detractor." Consider the power of creating thousands or millions of "promoters" of your product based upon delivering a "lights-out customer experience."

Many great companies use NPS scores regularly in their business—some even on a daily basis and some by individual restaurant or store. I recommend that any new business start tracking this NPS metric at the proof-of-concept stage. If this score is not significantly better than your competitors', then it's time to reconsider your business model. Once you move to the expansion stage of your company, it is important to continue tracking this metric. Valuable feedback for future action can be gleaned by asking one open-ended question to "The Ultimate Question": that is, "Why did you rate it that way?" These answers will give you insights into what is working and what is not from the customer's perspective.

It is not just a matter of tracking the NPS metric. It's also essential to share this and other key customer metrics regularly with everyone in your organization. These other metrics include the cost to acquire a customer, customer retention rates, and lifetime value of a customer. When these consumer metrics are highly visible, it sends the message that the consumer is the No. 1 priority.

Creating a lights-out customer experience, from my experience is THE most important strategy for business success. It's all about the customer. Create an amazingly satisfying customer experience, whether it's a product or a service. Elevate the quality of your customer experience so that it stands above every other competitor in your industry or category, and never violate what you stand for. **Make everything you do support an exceptional customer experience—from the design of the product or service to how you supply that product or service, to how you treat the customers after they've bought or used your product or service.** That means your customer satisfaction should be good enough to give you the confidence to expose the product or service—for businesses or consumers—to whatever people want to say about it. But you have to set the priority for customer experience so high, that it has to be at the top of the list of your first principles. Design everything around the customer experience: your value chain, the kinds of people you recruit, the priorities that you set for them, and how you reward and incentivize your team for success. All of those things should always lead back to a wonderful customer experience. Get that right to help make your business a big success.

PART IV

POWERFUL
TOOLS
FOR SUCCESS

1.

GETTING PREPARED TO BUILD

Genius is one percent inspiration and ninety-nine percent perspiration.

—Thomas Edison

To be in top form to build a successful business demands a rigor much like that of a high-performance athlete. Fortunately, not just the young can excel in this game. In fact, age and experience can be a decided plus. But getting in great shape both physically and mentally is really important to achieve focus and perform the hard work required of a successful entrepreneur or business builder. I eat well, work out regularly, and neither smoke nor drink. And I try to get a good night's sleep. That said, I work incredibly hard just about every day of the week. Why? Because I love to. Curiosity and passion drive me, and hard work is an essential ingredient in being successful. My brothers Arthur and David work as hard as I do because they love to as well. If it always seems like "work," then being a real business builder is probably not the spot for you.

Being in shape and working hard are important, but it's also valuable to think about preparation. At a recent dinner in Los Angeles, Lakers superstar Kobe Bryant and I were talking about preparation, and Kobe told me a riveting story. One of his trainers had told him that he would have to take a thousand shots a day if he really wanted to become a basketball great. Kobe said, "So I had to learn how to go out and do a thousand shots every day." He said: "When I started, the idea of a thousand shots every day seemed like an insurmountable number. I didn't know anybody who did a thousand shots a day and I finally got to the point where I could do a thousand shots every day." It didn't mean he got every one in, but he would shoot a thousand times. He said, "So I raised the bar: No one had ever done a thousand shots every day."

Innovators—including systemic designers and adaptive innovators—are a lot alike. They set very, very high goals because part of the way to succeed over other people is to raise the bar. Steve Jobs always was raising the bar. He had people doing things that they had no idea they were capable of doing, and he did it by seducing their minds, he did it by being brutally tough with them, humiliating them, whatever it took. But he got them to raise the bar. He had them in tears, he had them laughing, he had them exhausted, but he got them to do things beyond what they thought was even physically possible and they did it. That's how he got the Macintosh, and I assume that's how he got many of the other products that followed.

When you look at a brilliant athlete like Kobe Bryant, you might think, "Gee, he must just be able to coast now." No, he *still* does a thousand shots every day. As he explains that to younger players, they just stand there, he said, in amazement, and mutter with disbelief: "How can *anybody* do a thousand shots every day?"

If you want to change the world or build a transformative business, you have to invest the preparation time, like a superb athlete does. And you have to be driven by a noble cause. In the case of Kobe Bryant, he won't be satisfied with himself unless he demands everything of himself to be the very best basketball player in the world.

Entrepreneurs must be optimists. Thomas Edison maintained that he didn't fail a thousand times trying to find the best filament for an electric light bulb; he discovered a thousand filaments that wouldn't work. And Edison was an unstoppable action engine who believed "Everything comes to him who hustles while he waits." Today's innovators—no matter of what sort—have to speed ahead with the same energy and relentless determination. They also need a Moonshot mindset, a roadmap that will help put their ambitious goal within reach. That's what this book is designed to deliver.

2.

BE CURIOUS: ASK THE RIGHT QUESTIONS

The main thing that has caused companies to fail,
in my view, is that they missed the future.
> —Larry Page,
> cofounder and CEO, Google

INNOVATION STARTS
WITH FOCUSED LISTENING

Perhaps it was driven by irreverence for tradition, but in the early days of Apple, many of us used to make up our own job titles. My business card read "Chief Listener & CEO." It wasn't meant to be funny. It pretty accurately reflected an important part of a transformative CEO's roles. You need to be a skilled Listener and Decider. Effective observation and listening are incredibly important skills to learn.

As a youngster, I was constantly asking questions. I annoyed people like crazy because I wouldn't stop asking why things were the way they were. (I could be curious and explore a lot, because, when we lived on Long Island, there weren't many kids around to play with for quite a while.) Intense curiosity entails constantly observing, listening, and learning. Curiosity is not a recreational pastime. It's rooted in gaining a strategic advantage. Focused curiosity allows you to see possibilities before they become obvious. Intense curiosity is a trait I share with my brothers, and the three of us have been fortunate to leverage our curiosity into some successes in the business world.

Regularly reading key information sources is crucial to feeding my curiosity. I am up at 4:30 a.m. on most mornings to catch up on emails and check in on news sites like *Tech-Crunch*, *Business Insider*, and *Re/code*. Early mornings are when I do my "think" work and write important messages. At 6 a.m., I tune into *Squawk Box* and *Bloomberg Surveillance*. Bloomberg is more focused on tech news, but both are excellent shows. (Since I'm also involved with both personally, that also gives me an additional perspective on the news they cover. I'm a frequent guest host on Bloomberg, and I am invited to appear on *Squawk Box* several times a week, but I am often traveling or busy, so I typically appear on TV every week or two).

I try to look at a business opportunity from several different perspectives and make it a habit to stay up to date on business and financial news. I regularly read the *Financial Times*, *The Wall Street Journal*, *The New York Times*, and *The Economist*. I may use different publications as a lens for certain sorts of issues. For example, I rely on *The Wall Street Journal* less for its global view, and more for its expert coverage of U.S. industries, companies, and the state of business.

In this vast body of information, a given idea may be of no particular importance at the moment it's first encountered, but it will register later when I have more information and a clearer context. I am constantly scanning like a radar system—the web, emails I receive, and the several newspapers and magazines I read closely every day. I read at least part of lots of books. I have different "partners" in different business domains, often on a deal-by-deal basis. I like bouncing ideas off one of my partners or my wife, Diane, who is also my partner in our family office. So my life is, and always has been, very eclectic. I'm convinced that a billion-dollar business founder needs to have intense curiosity— the more wide-ranging in scope and the more purposeful in application, the better. The future belongs to those who see

possibilities before they become obvious. My operative hallmarks are: curiosity, listening, jotting down short notes in
my notebook, absorbing, searching for context, connecting,
collaborating, and reflecting. I love to road-test my ideas.
When I give interviews on television or speeches to various
groups, I am constantly road-testing ideas.

The founder of a billion-dollar business needs to be decisive, to be sure, but that decisiveness must also be coun-
terbalanced with testing and re-testing the vision in your
mind. This demands constant open-minded curiosity:

- Am I really open-minded to what my competition may
  be doing?
- Is the market *ready* for what I'm trying to do?
- Am I actually solving a billion-dollar problem?

Without constant and dedicated curiosity, you won't be
willing to adapt—all the way from the little tweaks to the
major adjustments. Is the penalty for insufficient curiosity
all that severe? Consider the following situation, and you be
the judge.

ASKING THE RIGHT QUESTION

Former Microsoft CEO Steve Ballmer was actually very successful transforming Windows applications from the PC to
the enterprise and competing with Oracle and IBM. But he
still managed to miss the opportunities of mobile, because
he insisted that Microsoft's mobile be a version of Windows.
PCs came from a different era. They were designed as knowledge worker tools. The user typically sat down and wasn't
bothered by a long boot cycle when the PC needed to be re-
started. Battery recharge cycle is also less important for a PC.
The operating norms that Microsoft assumed were acceptable belonged to the bygone PC era when Microsoft thrived,
and Microsoft became a victim of its own success. Apple
took a different path, building the best mobile smartphone

possible with no concern about compatibility with Mac software. Today, Microsoft's market cap is about $347 billion, versus Apple's at $579 billion and Microsoft's own historical market cap high of $616.3 billion in 1999. Apple took a creative leap with iPhone; Microsoft played it safe.

I haven't yet met the new Microsoft CEO, Satya Nadella, but I am impressed with one of his first strategy decisions: to put Windows Mobile apps on the Android and iOS platforms. In a single, history-reversing decision, what had previously been a sacred issue evaporated. Satya was now asking the right question: What can Microsoft do to be successful in mobile? Not the old question, "What can we do to make Windows Mobile a success?" Not much later, Satya followed up with another decision: Windows Mobile OS would be freely available for all mobile devices with a nine-inch or less screen size. To an outsider, one has to wonder what took them so long. Microsoft is filled with brilliant engineers, but, even in the smartest organizations, culture and ideology runs deep. Asking the right question often requires an objective open-mindedness that is difficult for many traditional CEOs. **Objectively looking at the facts is essential in combatting and overturning deeply ingrained cultures. This can be key for an adaptive innovator attempting to transform an existing organization.**

I wish I had been given the opportunity in high school to take a course about *how to learn*. What might such a course have included?

- Why questions are more important than answers.
- How to take notes.
- How to collaborate with other students.
- Why making mistakes and learning from them is more valuable than memorizing facts.
- How to think of a teacher as a mentor.

No such course existed then, and I know of no such course today. What an amazing void!

Asking the right questions is a really big idea—probably worth a book all by itself. A thoughtful, actionable examination could change the entire way we educate people. When I went to school, the emphasis was on "answers"—memorizing answers was how one was measured. **Today, we have pocket calculators, personal computers, Google, and Wikipedia; yet the education system around the world is still trapped in a model of answer preparation at a time when answers are just a commodity. The future of learning should be about asking the right questions.**

Schools are still trapped in a time warp of forcing kids to memorize facts and threatening expulsion for behavior that schools consider to be cheating. In school, if one talks to another student during a test, it's reviled as "cheating." In the real world, talking to a colleague in solving a problem is regarded as "collaboration." Something is wrong with this picture. Why isn't our education system organized around searching for the best "questions"? With the right questions, we have so many ways to get to the answers.

Let me describe another situation with great implications about how we learn, and you can decide if the lessons have true bottom-line significance.

What was the board of the former smartphone brand leader BlackBerry thinking? In a strategically perilous decision, they permitted their previous CEO, Thorsten Heins, to introduce the Z10 instead of updating the popular Black-Berry Bold smartphone launched in 2008.

Consider the situation when this decision was implemented: Apple's iOS and Google's Android already dominated the smartphone market, offering relatively similar user experiences. If you know how to use an iPhone, you'll feel pretty much at home using an Android phone too, with no special learning curve. No one was complaining that either iOS or Android were difficult to use. When the ground rules in the smartphone industry were significantly changed by Apple, Google, and Samsung, what did Black-Berry's board do? They decided BlackBerry had to come out with an entirely new, and what they believed to be, better operating system called QNX.

One result was that BlackBerry management eliminated the simplicity of a row of hardware buttons on the Bold and replaced it with an entirely new user experience that took days, even weeks, to learn. By failing to ask the right questions, BlackBerry deserted their most loyal customers, who were left waiting for better products. When the new Black-Berrys finally arrived, they were so different and complicated to learn that loyal users were appalled. They had no reward for patiently holding on for several years after Android and Apple redefined the mobile industry, expecting that new BlackBerry devices would rise to the challenge.

Thorsten Heins asked the wrong question. The question he tried to answer was: "How can BlackBerry create an up-to-date 'third way' operating system that is significantly different from iOS or Android?" Or, framed differently: "How can we create an even *better* and *different* user experience than the iPhone or Android mobile devices?"

But they asked the wrong questions. A better question might have been: "How can BlackBerry expand its highly regarded security service for regulated entities (e.g., financial services, lawyers, and government) into new regulated markets like health care?" Customers weren't looking for a better user interface than Android, they were looking for one that was *as good as* Android. In fact, it could even have *been* Android, as long as BlackBerry still had the best security, especially in a world where BYOD (bring your own device) had become the norm.

BlackBerry's new CEO, John Chen, is a very experienced turnaround executive who earned great praise in the high-tech industry for transforming failing Sybase into a better company that he later sold to SAP, reportedly for $5.8 billion. Imagine if BlackBerry's board had hired John Chen two years earlier? Since becoming BlackBerry's CEO, John Chen has moved rapidly to ask the right questions and make clear decisions. But the clock is ticking for BlackBerry following so many disastrous mistakes over the past few years. To compound the problems, BlackBerry was so overstaffed around the world that it became vulnerable to new competitors.

Asking the right question is anchored in a curious, open-minded, persevering approach. Perhaps even more important, it requires insight gained from looking at a problem from multiple points of view. These multiple viewpoints are at the heart of the next section, "Ground Yourself in Domain Expertise."

3.

GROUND YOURSELF
IN DOMAIN EXPERTISE

*Living in the same city as Microsoft, I'm only too aware that,
even in low-technology businesses like coffee, the Next Big
Thing could knock the dominant player into second place
tomorrow. I keep pushing to make sure that Starbucks thinks
of the Next Big Thing before it has even crossed anybody
else's mind.*

—Howard D. Schultz,
chairman and CEO, Starbucks

Domain expertise is fundamental to success. In his book
Outliers, Malcolm Gladwell emphasizes the "10,000-Hour
Rule" and uses the Beatles as a prime example. For Gladwell,
you need 10,000 hours of direct, hands-on experience to really qualify as an expert and do something special with your
skill. The Beatles got their 10,000 hours of intense experience playing together as a Liverpool rock band in Hamburg.
I'm not sure that 10,000 hours is the magic number you need
to qualify for domain expertise, but I am certain that an entrepreneur needs to be completely immersed in knowledge
about a sector to be able to create a billion-dollar business.

I can usually tell when someone is a recent graduate of
a top business school and did really well in the program.
These graduates are already generalizing the work that
they have done at business school. In MBA programs, you
typically get to look at lots of different cases, across lots of
different industries. Freshly minted MBAs usually *overvalue*
their technical skills in being able to analyze a business.

And they *undervalue* the nuts-and-bolts domain expertise that you need to amass in an industry.

Why is time in the trenches so important? When you're building a billion-dollar business, you will invariably hit bumps in the road. And you may even get to the point where your back is up against the wall. So often this can be prevented. If you have domain expertise, you'll recognize your problems sooner. You'll have more people to talk with in your network who can give you advice. If you need to replace somebody or add a new function, you'll know where to look faster. And you're going to understand the vernacular of the industry. Each industry has its own language, its own lexicon. And if you don't master the lexicon and use the wrong terms, it makes no difference how smart you are. You will be immediately devalued by everyone else in that domain area.

Marvin Minsky, an MIT Media Lab Artificial Intelligence professor, used to say, "You don't understand anything until you learn it more than one way." This is a game-changing insight. For existing companies, you can easily become a victim of your own success if you aren't tracking domains beyond your core competence. **Innovation almost always occurs first on the edges of an established industry. If you have only the one domain expertise that makes your company successful, you can easily become blindsided.**

An entrepreneur must be vigilant, always asking the questions: Who could encroach on the turf I want to stake out? Who is seeking to provide a similar customer result and/or experience? Be mindful that the source of that challenge may well be a totally different domain that seeks to expand its reach and/or applications in completely new areas. As technology advances, the prospect of incursions from unexpected sources rises exponentially. How many retailers, as one example, would have foreseen that Amazon, which began as a modest online bookstore twenty years ago, would today be redefining the entire profile and processes of the retail industry?

Domain expertise grounds your speculation in hard knowledge. With it, you can supplement what you know by zeroing in on exceptions. Over the years, I've recognized that the best way for me to learn things is like the peeling of the onion, but doing it backward. In other words, each layer of that onion skin is adding to the information base that I have. Today, I have enough knowledge of technology, enough knowledge of financial systems, and enough knowledge of various industry verticals that I can learn new information in a faster, more focused way. I think of it as analogous to a person who speaks several languages. After you become conversational in two or three, the next language you choose to learn becomes easier. When I read something, I don't have to remember the entire article. I can now read with a streamlined goal: Is there something different than what I knew about this before? So think of it as looking for the differences, not attempting to absorb all of the information.

Domain knowledge lets you look for the differences. Your focus becomes: What's different today from the last time I examined this subject? You can do that only if you build up knowledge layer by layer. This approach is quite unlike taking a subject, starting from scratch, and attempting to become an expert just by an accelerated, intensive investigation of that area. Instead, add to your knowledge base every day. Sometimes the addition may be just a tiny bit of knowledge. But it's day in/day out . . . day in/day out. Done over a period of months, even years, it's amazing how much you can deeply internalize about a subject.

Steadily, incrementally building domain knowledge gives you a formidable advantage. For example, I didn't get into health care until eight years ago. But since I made the decision to learn the domain, I've been thinking about health care every day for the past eight years. I still don't consider myself a domain expert in health care, but I have a lot more—and broader—knowledge than many people I meet who are actually in the sector. I know a lot about U.S. health care's illogical legacy regulations that have been foisted on the health care industry by special-interest lobbyists. I supplement that knowledge with my thirty years of high-technology domain expertise. I chose to focus my health care investments in the fast-developing patient-in-control sector, also known as the consumer era of wellness and sick care. This gives me a further advantage of leveraging my deep experience in consumer branding and marketing with the domains of high technology and health care. I have discovered that very few of us actually have experience in these three domains. It's a big advantage, and it helps get me a seat at the table with some of the best entrepreneurs. I may be able to see opportunities in connections between domains that are obscure to others. I look at the health care landscape very differently than the people who have been in health care their entire life. On intimate details, I will never know as much as they do about health care, but I will know it from a different angle. Sometimes, I will get an insight that may have been overlooked by professional health care experts just because their view is much narrower.

Here's an issue that certainly deserves attention: The U.S. has the best medicine and many of the best doctors in the world, with more than twice the per capita spending on health care of most other countries. Yet maybe 31.4 million or more of our people don't have health insurance. That's true even though the Affordable Care Act (also known as Obamacare) is one of the most expensive entitlement programs ever. Sounds complex, right? Actually, using domain expertise, we can unpack this question and see how creating a sustainable health system can be achieved. I have eight years of domain expertise in health care, so here's how I think about this question:

First, in the U.S. we reimburse doctors for the medical procedures they complete, not the outcomes of better wellness or sick care. Second, our largest cost of health care is in the last few months of a person's life and, unlike other countries, we will go to extraordinary efforts to keep someone alive no matter the cost. Five percent of the U.S. population represents our chronic care patients who typically suffer from multiple diseases and have five or more specialists taking care of them. The cost of chronic health care is approximately seventy-five percent of the $2.8 trillion spent on health care in the U.S. annually. Finally, in the U.S. our form of constitutional democracy creates powerful special interests, each having incredible influence. Consequently, there are carve-out agreements for pharmaceutical firms, unions, trial lawyers, doctors, insurance companies, government workers, military, and others that add huge expenses to our health care spending. Yes, it's very illogical and very complex in the details, as every state has different regulations.

Now think about the U.S. health care dilemma this way: If we take advantage of high technology and allow it to act as an intelligent assistant, we can shift a lot of the decider role to smarter consumers, who also will in turn become smarter patients. For example, CMS (the U.S. Medicare and Medicaid agency) estimates that as many as seventy percent of face-to-face doctor visits could be handled remotely online. Obesity is an epidemic. If every American would lose twenty pounds, our health system could save billions of dollars a year. Remember those chronic care patients that are five percent of the population but represent most of our health care spending? If we can reduce obesity, we will likely reduce type 2 diabetes significantly too. There is a well-known chain reaction of comorbidities between chronic diseases. Reduce type 2 diabetes and we will likely significantly reduce other chronic diseases like sleep apnea, congestive heart failure, COPD, hypertension, and depression. **Change your point of view about health care from treating events to understanding wellness and sick care as customer-centric, end-to-end systems. Think about how we can influence smarter patients to become deciders in their own wellness, and new possibilities can emerge.**

HEALTH CARE'S LARGEST COMPANY
ADDS A NEW DOMAIN EXPERTISE

Optum is a $38 billion division of United Health Group, the largest private-enterprise supplemental health system in the U.S. In 2014, Optum acquired an early-stage private company called Audax Health Solutions, founded by an extremely talented twenty-five-year-old, Grant Verstandig. One effect of the Affordable Care Act is that U.S. employers, who have traditionally been the health insurance firms' largest clients, are changing over to a self-insured employer business model. As these self-insured employers take on the insurance risk pool of their own employees, they must offer many new wellness services for their employees and families. It's a great opportunity for Optum to have a game-changing moment. United Health Group's CFO, Dave Wichmann, for a long time a very successful adaptive innovator at this health giant, saw an opportunity for a better way to serve self-insured employers by offering their employees a range of much improved wellness and sick care solutions. The key was building a consumer-branded engagement service, Optum, that its employees would actually use. Optum was already an expert in health care and high technology, but Dave Wichmann wanted to add a new domain of creative social media expertise.

Audax had built the best consumer engagement software engine in the industry, targeting female heads of household and presenting these women with a very user-friendly health risk assessment tool. Audax combined this with virtual communities-of-interest, a system of wellness goals, tracking, and rewards with engaging wellness-related online games, as well as many new supplemental health services. Consumers love the service, and, since becoming a part of Optum, Audax has been scaling rapidly. Why has Audax been so successful at consumer engagement while others have tried hard to do this and failed? Grant Verstandig built his company around three different expertise domains: the complex regulations of legacy health care, automated intelligent software engines incorporating Big Data analytics, and some of the best Silicon Valley creative talent with consumer games and social media experience. At Audax, customers come first and customers are now the deciders of many of their most important wellness decisions. Audax is now able to offer consumers high-value, online coaching services for issues like anxiety, weight loss, stress, fitness, smoking cessation, drug addiction, and more. It's a huge success.

I like health care because it's a noble cause with many big, juicy, billion-dollar problems needing solutions. These are perfect opportunities for adaptive innovators if they have access to the right domain expertise.

Alan Kay was one of my closest advisers at Apple. He was an Apple Fellow, a child prodigy who at the age of eleven appeared on a radio show called *Quiz Kids*, which challenged young geniuses with really hard puzzles to solve. Alan Kay was also the first computer scientist at Xerox PARC to envision a truly personal computer—a device he described as the "Dynabook." Of course, nobody could actually build a Dynabook in 1971, but Alan—working on a giant minicomputer like DEC's PDP-11—went on to develop the first object-oriented programming language called SmallTalk. Alan used to say, "Point of view is worth 80 IQ points." This was another way of expressing Marvin Minsky's insight that I mentioned earlier: You don't really understand something until you understand it more than one way.

After I left Apple in 1993, I got to know Professor Howard Gardner at Harvard's School of Education. Howard's discoveries about the multiple kinds of human intelligence are truly amazing. He considers IQ a very simplistic way to think about human intelligence. Howard believes we actually have competences in multiple intelligences, from logic, to intuition, to design, to eye-hand coordination, as with a skilled athlete like Kobe Bryant shooting a basketball into a hoop. Each form of intelligence is a different way to process information. **Just as multiple domains are important, having multiple ways to think about a problem and process information is important too.** We don't all do it the same way.

Extending your range of domain expertise multiplies your ability to detect opportunities, especially those that interrelate categories with a base of drastic change. Obvious advantages emerge when you've been tracking a domain for decades. I've seen high technology transformed in many different waves, from the Personal Computer Era, to the Internet Era, to the Cloud Era, and now to the Mobility Era. That's technology as seen through many different contexts. It's appreciating context that makes this information useful. When I look at consumer marketing, I can apply a long history of working with brand building in all kinds of consumer products. So I have an edge identifying opportunities in either high technology or consumer branding, and I have an even better advantage when the topic is consumer branding *of* high technology. My advantage boils down to a slowly acquired apprenticeship in the gathering and use of specialized information. In a nutshell: **Multiple-domain expertise can be more valuable than cool technology.**

TAKING DEEP DIVE IMMERSIONS

Sometimes you have to supplement even domain expertise. If you hope to transform a domain, you can't just skirt along the surface. You need to be able to take deep dives. Deep-dive analysis is an information immersion for a person or a team to blitz-learn an industry sector from top to bottom. An enormous help to a deep dive is having a mentor or partner, truly an expert in the domain, whom you can trust to shortcut the immersion and focus you on the most critical goals. "Deep dives" can be a truly exhilarating experience, especially when one goes into this process with an overarching curiosity to define the right questions. Your goal is to study the same facts that others have accepted and maybe undervalued in a different context, and to try identifying something in these facts that wasn't previously fully appreciated.

Grounding yourself in domain expertise is invaluable for transformative success in building businesses. Most innovation isn't totally original. This is why domain expertise is so important. *Aha!* moments come when one adapts insights from different domains. While having multiple domains in your personal toolkit are sometimes difficult credentials to acquire—particularly if you are young—having an organization with expertise in multiple domains is essential. As you will see in the next chapter, the solution to mastering domain expertise often involves "putting the right people on the bus."

4.

PUT THE RIGHT PEOPLE ON THE BUS

*A company should limit its growth based on
its ability to attract enough of the right people.*
  —Jim Collins,
       management consultant
       and author, *Good to Great*

Building the business is all about building the best team.

Put the right people on the bus and make sure you have them positioned in the right seats. Be frugal about many things, but not about the quality of the people you will accept on your team. Admit and shore up your own weaknesses. Complement yourself with a team. Great companies are built by great teams. They aren't built by just one person.

For me, I've also long had a simple rule that has been easy to implement, since I enjoy interacting with people with different viewpoints, provided they have strong personal values (like integrity), demonstrate a passion for their work, and are committed to doing a good job: I work only with people I like. Compromising on your team ultimately means: "I'm willing to compromise with my customer in their customer experience." Few mistakes can be more costly than that. **If you don't have the correct team in place to undertake a particular strategy, improvising a launch in a new direction can prove risky and regrettable.**

When you hire your team, your mission is not to clone yourself. It's to build the talent mix you'll need to steer the business. Sure, you want to have shared values and a commonly held vision. **Entrepreneurs who have built billion-dollar businesses likely didn't do it with cookie-cutter teams. Rather, they harness unique horsepower by hiring people with complementary talents to take the business to the moon.** Start by inventorying your own weaknesses and determine how you need to supplement and compensate for those shortcomings if the business is to be successful.

You'll need people who are different than you and quite possibly smarter than you. Certainly they'll be smarter in certain areas. My brothers Arthur and David and I enjoy working together. All three of us have been CEOs at one time. David is the youngest, and he's also the one best suited to handle people management issues and oversee day-to-day operations of the business. I may be good at generating ideas and figuring out systemic solutions to problems and opportunities, whereas my brother Arthur has amazing international and financial services expertise. I may be more publicly recognized than my brothers, but it's David who does the heavy lifting of people and process managing. I'm an adaptive innovator who builds with ideas. David is a builder too, but he has the talent and patience to build and manage the complexity of actually running a business. These are different skills; both important to success.

Another thing about the Sculley brothers: We like to get things done. We don't waste time arguing; we just get along. We grew up in a loving home where modesty was a virtue. I remember once coming home and telling my mother I had just been promoted to be a vice president at Pepsi. She said, "That's nice, dear. Would you please take out the garbage?" And we love the assertion variously attributed to Ronald Reagan and Harry Truman among others, "It's amazing what you can accomplish if you do not care who gets the credit." Focus on the job you need to do and align the talent to get it done.

For a variety of convincing reasons, founders often come in pairs. In the high-tech world, some of the most successful companies had two founders. Why? Because one may have done more than the other in another domain or another aspect of the same domain. They supplemented each other. Often, their skills complemented each other. You also get the chance to bounce ideas off each other. You may have two cofounders and sometimes you'll have more than two cofounders: No company is built by one person. One of the founders will be stronger at being able to define the business, the vision, and the mission, and to inspire people. Another founder may be better at getting it done. It usually takes at least those two different mindsets.

In the most legendary Silicon start-up of all, Bill Hewlett and David Packard founded Hewlett-Packard in a one-car Palo Alto garage in 1939.

Bob Noyce and Gordon Moore founded Intel.

Bill Gates and Paul Allen founded Microsoft.

Steve Jobs and Steve Wozniak founded Apple.

And the practice of cofounding continues down to the present day. Brian Chesky, CEO of Airbnb, cofounded the original concept in 2007 with Joe Gebbia, who is today chief product officer. This team quickly added a third cofounder when the business was actually launched in 2008: Nathan Blecharczyk, today chief technical officer.

Appreciate the advantage of people being able to talk to each other, to challenge each other's thinking, even to mentor each other. There may have been two cofounders, but there's one person who's making the big decisions. And that's for a very good reason: Innovation is not done by consensus. Somebody has to make decisions, and it's okay for some of those decisions to be wrong. Democracy doesn't work when you're running an intensely innovative business, especially a high-tech one. There has to be one decider. That's something Steve Jobs felt passionately about, and I do, too.

A good, creatively charged team gives you amazing

latitude. The best overall manager that Apple had while I was there, in my opinion, was Del Yocam. After experience at Ford Motor and Control Data, Del joined Apple in 1979 and became Apple's first COO (chief operating officer) in the late 1980s, while I was CEO. On his tenth anniversary at Apple, he retired from the company and later went on to realize a spectacular turnaround at Tektronix in Oregon.

It's not unusual for founder CEOs of a business to be both highly visionary and intensely detail-conscious and controlling. To make sure that the vision is actually executed requires the capacity to flip between those two modes with nonstop energy and unending flexibility. Many entrepreneur/founders will constantly find ways to intrude in every detail of the business. At Google, Larry Page had several simple rules that will serve many entrepreneurs well as they manage others. One of the most formidable was: "Don't get in the way if you're not adding value. Let the people actually doing the work talk to each other while you go do something else."

Speaking of Google, Thomas Friedman, the brilliant global columnist for *The New York Times*, wrote a fascinating piece in February 2014 entitled, "How to Get a Job at Google." He reports on an interview between Adam Bryant of *The Times* and Google's senior vice president for people, Laszlo Bock. Bock notes that the percentage of Google employees without a college education is growing. The reason? Google learned that there is no correlation between college grades and success at Google. The skills they are looking for in new employees relate to functioning well in a group environment: "soft skills—leadership, humility, collaboration, adaptability and loving to learn and re-learn." Successful new companies today are empowering project teams with different sorts of domain expertise who can collaborate effectively. As you start putting the right people on the bus, it makes sense to consider the types of skills that Google has found to be essential for its success.

To reiterate, recognize the kind of talent you need, at each stage of building your billion-dollar business. Have the right people on the bus, in terms of a management team, and then you have them sitting on the right seats on the bus. Remember that the right seats may change as the business evolves and as the aspirations of key players mature. As you recruit the talent pool you need to deliver on your mission, don't overlook a valuable source of recommendations. In more and more companies, new recruits are recommended by existing employees. Networking existing staff to find new recruits is much likelier to find you people with kindred values and objectives, although you want to be sure that this kind of staffing doesn't make your talent mix too homogeneous. Finally, keep your management hierarchy shallow. You want as few levels as possible between founder/top management and the battlefield positions actually interacting with customers, writing programming code, or cooking up product in the lab.

AGE: QUITE POSSIBLY AN ADVANTAGE

The best wine may indeed be maturing in old bottles. Despite considerable evidence to the contrary, the conventional wisdom abides that innovation and entrepreneurship are the sole province of the young. The assumption is simply untrue. Films like *The Social Network* sell well into the Millennial demographic, but they hardly tell the whole story about who's cranking out the bulk of business innovation.

The age at which entrepreneurs are more innovative and willing to take risks seems to be going up. According to data from the Kauffman Foundation, the highest rate of entrepreneurship in America has shifted to the fifty-five-to-sixty-four age group, with people over fifty-five almost twice as likely to found successful companies than those between twenty and thirty-four. And while the entrepreneurship rate has gone up since 1996 in most other age brackets as well, it has actually declined among Americans under thirty-five.

A revealing article by Noam Scheiber in *The New Republic*

notes that "older people have historically been just as 'disruptive' as younger people." The creator of Internet apps for consumers, according to Scheiber, averages out to be thirty-four years old. For no good reason at all, Scheiber observes, "we now have a large and growing class of highly trained, objectively talented, surpassingly ambitious workers who are shunted to the margins, doomed to haunt corporate parking lots and medical waiting rooms, for reasons no one can rationally explain." A vast reservoir of experienced, older talent is available to either launch start-ups or to find seats on the bus in making them happen.

FINDING THE RIGHT PEOPLE IS A NEW BUSINESS IN ITSELF

A dramatically different sort of billion-dollar business opportunity is a personnel services venture catalyzed by dramatic innovations that first emerged in real estate. Zillow is the real estate industry's trusted and online automated expert system, which quickly tells a consumer or a real estate professional what different type homes in a neighborhood should cost based on comparable transactions. Zillow completely changed the real estate industry.

Back in 2002, a *Fast Company* magazine contributing editor named Daniel Pink published a book titled *Free Agent Nation* discussing "the future of working for yourself." He recognized that professional athletes were not the only "free agents" in our world of work. Even a decade ago, 25 million people were self-employed. In this new "microbusiness" world, a major missing feature has been systematic approaches that far more efficiently match supply and demand.

Why not do for skilled people what Zillow did for real estate? Joe Musacchio, a wonderful friend of mine, is one of the entrepreneurs I mentor, and he is founder and CEO of a new company named "PeopleTicker." This is a free online service that tells people how much they are worth. Think of PeopleTicker as the Zillow equivalent for skilled workers who are qualified and willing to work on a project-consulting basis. This is just one segment of the free-agent nation, but a very important one. There were 10.3 million such people in the U.S. workforce in 2005. In 2013, there were 17 million skilled part-time workers employed as outside contractors in the U.S. According to *Forbes* in 2013, that's a third of the nation's workforce already, and outside contractors will outnumber full-time employees by 2019! What used to be a bridge job between permanent-employment spots is becoming a career of choice for many today. Keep your eye on this trend; it will inevitably become more important.

Joe has amassed 200 million profiled jobs—corporate and freelance—and is able to tell anyone, based on you entering your skills and experience, what you are worth in any city in North America. Temporary workers, many of whom are highly skilled with excellent work experience, are willing, and often even prefer, to be independent contractors. They choose to work for clients on a project basis rather than seeking full-time employment. These workers are a growing part of America's workforce, creating a flexible and very adaptable employment alternative.

Many in People Ticker's talent pool come from the cadre of knowledge workers first described by Peter Drucker. These knowledge workers drove the world economy during the era of globalization in the 1980s and 1990s. Some of them are the same knowledge worker casualties being eliminated by corporate re-engineering, virtualization, and outsourcing, by cloud computing, smart robots, and predictive analytics. Others choose project-based consulting, often from their homes, as a lifestyle decision.

PeopleTicker is a people stock exchange for a free-agent nation. It's evolving into one of the most important contingent skilled labor information services in the world, and it's a beautiful example of a potential billion-dollar company that's responding to the very dislocation being caused by the technological tsunami in which we are immersed.

Putting the right people on the bus is critical to the success of a transformative new business. Over time, the destination of the business may well change. Sometimes the people on the bus need to move to new seats as the business grows. Sometimes early hires cannot adapt to a company that moves beyond proof of concept or to later stages of expansion. These can be hard decisions, as are the ones to bring in new talent from other domains. But they are essential and unavoidable for a business to remain viable.

5.

ZOOMING

Simplicity is the ultimate perfection.
—Steve Jobs

Adaptive innovators will find "zooming" to be a tool of extraordinary power. Steve Jobs and I typically took a walk together almost every day. When Steve would say, "John, let's take a walk," I knew he was thinking his way through a new idea or he was trying to unpack the complexity of ideas already in some stage of development. Sometimes we would walk around Apple's small campus in Cupertino and end up at Steve's favorite eating place, The Good Earth restaurant. Other times, we would go over to Stanford University and walk around their beautiful campus. On weekends, we might climb Windy Hill, a steep open space that leads up to Skyline Boulevard, with its impressive views of Silicon Valley looking back to the east or westward to the Pacific Ocean.

It was on these many walks that I learned one of Steve Jobs' most useful personal tools, one he called "zooming." Its starts first with the "zoom out," an overview scan across different unrelated domains. Steve fell in love with calligraphy when he was briefly a student at Reed College, and that interest underpinned one of his most spectacular applications of zooming out. Years after the Apple II had been launched, Woz, Steve, and Apple engineer Jef Raskin were invited to visit Xerox PARC (Palo Alto Research Center) near Stanford. On this fateful visit, PARC computer scientist Larry Tesler showed his Apple visitors the STAR and Alto graphics-based computer prototypes that Xerox was creating in the lab. PARC was a research center, not a commercial products group, and the prototype machines would probably have been priced at $25,000 or even more when fully configured.

When Steve Jobs returned to Apple, he was totally psyched, because he had just seen the future. But it was a different future than the one PARC scientists were creating. Steve Jobs wanted to build a graphics-based personal computer as the world's first really easy-to-use media machine, a device that could be priced about the same as an Apple II at $2,500. To do this was going to take the best of Woz's improvisational wizardry as a hacker. Otherwise, the technology to do what Steve Jobs envisioned might be a decade away. When the Mac was finally introduced in January 1984, our marketing theme was "There has to be a better way." And we were specifically referring to the ability for nontechnical people to have their own affordable and easy-to-use desktop publishing system.

Zooming to create a better way to solve a billion-dollar problem is a yin-yang solution. After *zooming out* and connecting the dots as Steve Jobs did when he conceptualized the Mac, one then has to *zoom in* and simplify everything. Steve would point out to me that *the hardest decisions are not what to put in, but what to leave out.* Mark Twain once apologized in a letter to a friend that he was sorry he had written such a long letter as he didn't have time to write a shorter one. In the decade that I was at Apple, I saw many examples of really talented companies falling into the trap of not simplifying and succumbing to what we called "feature creep."

Feature creep has claimed many illustrious victims in

business, especially in high tech. After the untimely death of Sony cofounder Akio Morita, who had created the brilliant and very simple Sony Walkman, Sony lost its way and ended up making thousands of undistinguished consumer products, each with way too many features. Sony lost its magic. Years later, it was Steve Jobs, long a Sony admirer in the early 1980s when Akio Morita was in charge, who created the successor to the Walkman. It was, of course, the iPod and iTunes, a complete end-to-end music download system and service combined. If Akio Morita had lived, my guess is he would have understood the power of zooming out and then zooming in to simplify the consumer experience in every possible way, and might well have arrived at a solution comparable to the iPod.

Zooming is even more relevant today, as the four exponential digital technologies of the cloud, wireless sensors, Big Data, and mobile devices are combined with the incredible fast-to-scale power of the network effect. This combination of resources makes it very affordable to connect the dots between otherwise unrelated areas of different kinds of domain expertise, making it ever easier to identify transformative business opportunities.

A few insights I have found really useful: As a transformative entrepreneur, your team must become seriously knowledgeable and competent in more than one domain. Even if you aren't totally competent in all the relevant domains, you must be able to meaningfully zoom out and connect the dots of the bigger picture. With team members who are experts in all the relevant domains, you will have both the expertise and the technology tools to design disruptive and better ways to do something.

6.

BACK FROM THE FUTURE PLANNING

There are two ways to extend a business. . . . Take inventory of what you're good at and extend out from your skills. Or determine what your customers need and work backward, even if it requires learning new skills. Kindle is an example of working backward.

—Jeff Bezos,
founder and CEO, Amazon

CREATING 10× SOLUTIONS

Larry Page, cofounder of Google, has challenged his employees to find 10× solutions—answers that are ten times better than the competition. This means solutions that will be ten times better than how people do that task today, if it can even be done at all today. Often a 10× better goal will be a combination of a better customer experience with other key factors. The mix could include a disruptive price, a different way of delivering that product or service, or offering a complete alternative substitute that is cheaper, faster, better, and more convenient.

Google calls this creative process "Solve for ×." Conceptualize what might be possible without actually breaking the laws of physics. And when you speculate with such dramatically different possibilities, never forget that a 10× solution may not be feasible or implementable near term.

When we think about "there has to be a better way," it isn't simply about improving something. Jeff Bezos clearly achieved a 10× goal when he created Amazon. He created an entirely new way of thinking about the sale and delivery of all kinds of goods and services. We are now in the era where brick-and-mortar retail and online commerce have collided by integrating mobility, more and more data analytics, and the ability of knowing exactly who buys what, when, and where. We're going to see 10× goal businesses emerge from this collision point of contact.

It's totally realistic to expect that some exceptional 10× businesses will be created over the next five years. They will be multibillion-dollar companies with very recognizable brand names, and they're going to happen all over the world; it won't just be in Silicon Valley.

Google's "Solve for ×" and Larry Page's emphasis on 10× solutions may have originated in Silicon Valley and been promoted successfully by brilliant people at Google, but the reality is that the concept is ready for prime time all over the world. These exponential technologies of cloud, mobility, sensors, and Big Data science are now very available and affordable to almost anybody who wants to build a billion-dollar business. Add to that the network effect that means everything and everyone is connected. Disruptive, creative 10× concepts able to solve billion-dollar problems in novel ways can turn into real companies very quickly. That wasn't possible even five or six years ago.

WHY THE BUSINESS PLANNING CONCEPT IS DYING

Have you ever pondered why next year's business plan takes months to prepare and is usually a very detailed document filled with assumptions and supporting analysis; yet it's almost always possible to explain what happened last year in just one or two pages? The difference is that one is looking forward with assumptions about unknowns, while the other is looking back at what actually happened.

Typically, business executives look at annual planning in the traditional way. They say: "Here's where I am. Let's build

a roadmap for things I'm working on and project them going forward. That should tell me where I'll be at the end of
this year, next year, and the year after."

These long, detailed plans often take months of preparation and require presentations consuming thousands of
hours of management time. While the financials are usually consolidated and reported, the massive planning documents themselves are rarely looked at again. What a wasted
exercise! If a company wants to become a transformative
adaptive corporation, I believe it should focus on a customer
plan, instead of the conventional business plan. **A customer
plan should be a concise document outlining how the
company will significantly improve the customer experience to make it the best by far in your industry.** At
the heart of the customer plan is a planning tool I have used
over and over again in my business career, called Back From
the Future Planning.

The starting point for Back From the Future Planning
is your 10× goal—even if that 10× goal is four years in the
future. If your goal is further out than that, then you are
probably at too early a stage to know what's possible.
Network-effect businesses scale fast enough that planning
for the first four years is ample for most new companies.
A few years ago, that time horizon might have been five to
seven years.

When Steve Jobs reinvented photography with the
iPhone, his vision brought together several emerging realities. In 2007, the world was shifting from the text-centered
world of 2G wireless to 3G wireless, which was far more
photo-friendly. By 2007, it was possible to take a photo and
send it wirelessly on a then-advanced mobile phone. Steve
Jobs took advantage of the dramatic drop in cost of the consumer electronic components, since the consumer electronics industry a decade earlier had switched to digital,
largely for music devices. He didn't invent digital photography and he didn't invent generic MP3 music players. But he
adapted these inventions from others and ended up getting

all the spoils. At times, Steve Jobs was a successful systemic designer. At other times, he was an equally effective adaptive innovator.

Steve Jobs zoomed out and connected the dots and saw that it would be possible to take a picture on a mobile device. You could instantly look at it. You could send it wirelessly over 3G to a Mac or to a Windows PC and post the photo on the web. You could then print it with a printer connected to a PC, and you could build all kinds of apps that leveraged off of the imaging capabilities of the iPhone. After that, photography was never the same.

There will be 10x companies started this year or next that will have 10x goals and be household names four years later. Such companies could be the next Uber, Airbnb, or WhatsApp. They might also be new B2B services in health care that combine different domain expertise from independent companies. Companies like Salesforce.com believe they see just such an opportunity to work on connected health solutions combining their respective domain expertise.

HOW BACK FROM THE FUTURE PLANNING WORKS

Back From the Future Planning starts with a possible 10x goal and the intent to turn the possible into probable. That's manageable only if you think sequentially with concrete goals. Start at four years out and then step back, quarter by quarter, listing the few very important things that must happen in each quarter. If one does this for the full four years, that's sixteen quarters matched with a limited number of achievable tasks. The first few times you try this approach, in all likelihood you'll be disappointed by the time you get all the way back to the present. The things that must get done in the first year will seem more impossible than probable. That's because you'll be looking at the magnitude of what you need to do in a realistic way with a plausible calendar.

This exercise underscores that disruption is hard and

that it's very different than a performance improvement plan. You need to get your head into a very different frame of mind. That's why adaptive innovators are so significant. They occupy key positions because they have the skills to get good stuff done by adapting the rules, thinking outside the box, not focused on "no," but focused on "yes." Such talent is usually essential for a start-up to even survive. For established companies that are already successful, no one may be identified in the adaptive innovator role, or the person chosen for this role has the wrong domain expertise to do the job successfully. In very successful companies, deploying the best executive stars to 10× transformative missions may seem like squandering talent. In fact, it may be their best possible use.

The customer plan that utilizes Back From the Future Planning does not have to result in a long, wordy document like a traditional business plan. It *does* need to have a clear, bold, and concise goal—usually built around a vision to reinvent an existing business category or industry that delivers a consumer experience never seen before and preferably at a disruptive price. A meaningful customer plan needs to have simplified end-to-end systems, leveraging today's exponential technologies, identified at least in concept, to deliver the goal. And the plan should have an easy-to-understand quarterly flowchart of key milestones. As the projects required to deliver the vision become clearer, appropriate resources, including possible acquisitions, can be identified in more detail.

Back From the Future Planning is a useful tool, I believe, for adaptive innovators to deliver on Clayton Christensen's formidable concept of "Disruptive Innovation." **A worthwhile measure to apply: If the end result isn't about growing in new ways from new sources of growth, then you are in a sustaining growth business, not transformative growth.**

But what happens, even with the best plan, when your business hits a big bump and your back is against the wall?

It happens all the time, even to the most successful entrepreneurs. And what happens if you fail? It has certainly happened to me. That is the topic for my next section: How to
Pivot When Your Back Is Against the Wall.

7.

HOW TO PIVOT WHEN
YOUR BACK
IS AGAINST THE WALL

People who don't take risks generally make about two big mistakes a year. People who do take risks generally make about two big mistakes a year.
                    —Peter F. Drucker,
                        management expert

David Steinberg, CEO of the digital Big Data marketing firm Zeta Interactive, is one of my closest friends, and we co-founded this company together. David is a very experienced serial entrepreneur. He is also a master of how to pivot. **Why is pivot zone expertise so important? Because many, perhaps most, entrepreneurial businesses will find themselves thrown into at least one life-threatening situation where they will need to sharply fine-tune or completely redefine themselves to survive.**

The name of the company when we originally founded it was XL Education, and it was an online lead-generation company designed to acquire students for 300 higher education institutions. Nicely profitable after a few years, having achieved an annual volume of $75 million, XL Education hit a wall, not of David's making, as several powerful leaders in the U.S. Congress went on the attack against for-profit higher education institutions. They felt that students were taking on too much student-loan indebtedness.

The student-loan business sector was thrown into upheaval, and David needed to completely redefine his business. He went into his "pivot zone" and accomplished one of the most remarkable pivots I have seen an entrepreneur make. David shifted his core business into a customer acquisition and marketing data analytics firm targeting mortgages, insurance, and credit card users. He identified a completely new application that could benefit from his domain expertise and core talent base.

The pivot was by no means easy or painless:

- David laid off seventy percent of his employees.
- He raised almost $50 million to undertake the transition.
- He made four very smart small-company acquisitions, including the purchase of a back-office business process outsourcer in India.

The successor business, which we renamed Zeta Interactive, emerged as an incredibly well positioned, high-growth marketing firm. Not all pivots are as drastic as David's, but all entrepreneurs should arm themselves with the same flexibility and open-mindedness that David put to good use.

Zeta Interactive is immersed in Big Data analytics for customer life-cycle management. Optimized in mining data around 340 million profiled names and spearheaded by thirty-nine PhD data scientists in Hyderabad, India, Zeta specializes in customer acquisition, customer loyalty, and the monetizing of customer relationships. Today, in my opinion, Zeta Interactive has a good chance of being worth well over $1 billion in the next few years.

This was not David Steinberg's first time with his back against the wall. He learned big-time lessons at the previous company he founded, InPhonic, which had early success, but years later filed for bankruptcy. This experience helped turn him into a true world-class business leader. In 1999, he founded InPhonic, which sold mobile phones online. At first, the company was successful, and in a few years had an IPO and a market cap of over a billion dollars as a public company.

Later, facing a changing telecommunications market, In-Phonic was forced to voluntarily reorganize under Chapter 11. David was forced to sell much of InPhonic to a distressed fund acquirer. Here was David, only months earlier a rock star in the high-tech community—and then, suddenly the press was hounding him as a failure.

Throughout this experience, InPhonic was always loyal to its customers and continued to run as smoothly as it could, given the cash-crunch pressures. Nevertheless, class-action law suits piled up. Several board members and key executives resigned. Life in the fast lane is not without risks, but David rebounded expertly, and the skills he learned were later essential in the ultimate success today of Zeta Interactive. In the high-technology world especially, and in business start-ups generally, failure can put you on a rocky emotional roller coaster, and you have to learn to hang on. David Steinberg's story is a modern classic of an entrepreneur pivoting his way from setback to success.

Another really good friend of mine, Dan Gittleman, Open-Peak founder and CEO, was building a tablet device firm when Apple came out with the iPad and completely took over the market. What to do? Dan is an experienced serial entrepreneur, having sold his last company, StoreApps, to HP for more than $300 million. Dan knew not to give up. He thought about what other really big customer problems he could solve that would take advantage of OpenPeak's intellectual property and his talented software team. After a few months of study, Dan came up with the answer. His software technology was perfect for solving the BYOD (bring your own device) problem that enterprises encountered as they allowed their employees to use their own smartphones for both personal and business data. This presented a real security risk unless addressed properly. Several firms were already building mobile-device management solutions, but none of the competition had the deep wireless carrier domain expertise that Dan Gittleman's team had. OpenPeak has added important innovations that became highly valued by wireless carriers, like the ability to have two phone numbers, one personal and the other business, on the same mobile device. It's now several years later and OpenPeak has forged strategic partnerships with AT&T, SAP, and many wireless carriers around the world. Dan Gittleman's pivot is a great story of what an adaptive innovator can do when your back is against the wall.

Recently, I got to spend time with an incredible entrepreneur, Leslie Blodgett, executive chairman of Bare Escentuals. Leslie is one of the biggest success stories in the cosmetics industry. After many years of experience in the cosmetics industry, Leslie joined a small retail business, Bare Escentuals, as CEO in 1994. The firm only had seven or eight employees and almost no revenue. It owned a few boutiques that sold bath and beauty products, mainly around the holidays. By 1996, Leslie knew the business model wasn't working very well, and she was concerned the company wouldn't survive.

This is when Leslie created an amazing pivot. Her background in large cosmetics companies had been in makeup. She was convinced that Bare Escentuals needed to refocus in this category. She looked at a little-known item in the Bare Escentuals line—a powder foundation—and focused development on this one product. She made another move that proved to be game changing. With absolutely no television experience, she applied to be a spokeswoman for bareMinerals on QVC. This was back when cosmetics were promoted by professional models and actresses.

But Leslie knew how to explain makeup and skin tones in a way that was easy for QVC's female viewers to relate to. The rest is history, with Bare Escentuals a huge success. Leslie sold it to the Japanese giant Shiseido in 2010 for $1.7 billion. It all started, however, with her successful pivot.

Another great example of a successful pivot is Netflix, which was founded as a mail-order company lending and selling movies on DVD to subscribers. Then the mail-order business began to be disrupted by media streaming over the Internet. Netflix, like many companies that seek to reinvent their business model, experienced trouble making the shift to an on-demand movie-delivery business. Its stock dropped from a high of $300 to $53 in 2012 as consumers began shifting their TV watching behavior to watching *what* they wanted *when* they wanted to see it—a far cry from traditional network television and its appointment program viewing.

Then Netflix successfully pivoted to online movie distribution on demand. And then Netflix produced thirteen hours of on-demand original programing, *House of Cards*, and rented movies and TV programs for a very attractive price of $8.99 a month. While Netflix's traditional customers for mail order were 10 million U.S. subscribers, the Internet streaming pivot reached out to viewers beyond the U.S. Netflix's expanded audience today is more than 48 million viewers. The stock has gone from $53 in 2012 to over $400 per share.

A rebound is rarely a rigid, persistent, straight-line bounce-back retracing the same direction as the decline. Time and again, pivoting has been the springboard to entrepreneurial success. Learn your pivot zone and how to master it, because the return to success is nearly never a 180-degree comeback or turnaround. To appreciate the potential power of your pivot zone, you need to start by examining your risk-taking behavior and how you handle failure.

MANAGING RISK

Most entrepreneurs are natural risk-takers. It's inherent in the attitude of wanting to do things in a better way and being willing to try something different. However, learning how to embrace risk intelligently can be a different matter.

Breadth of experience gives risk-taking a great edge. Do

you know the boundaries of how much change can actually be implemented without risk of hurting the company? How do you know, as a person, if you've never worked in a different industry or in a different company? You can only grasp the importance of this, I think, by being curious and by constantly looking around. Pay attention to what competitors are doing. Look at other industries and imagine a similar scenario playing out in your competitive world. Be willing to say, "That could happen in my industry, too." The disruption might be something that is detrimental, or it might be something that opens up an entirely new realm of opportunity.

Risks can be reduced by getting your timing right. This is hard, particularly when you are shaping a new market. **You can help limit the impact of timing risks by controlling how quickly and extensively you build your expense base. Whenever possible, practice frugal spending, maintain a lean organization, and stay virtual until you have demonstrated a proof of concept.** Timing can pose pivotal risks that argue for vigilance.

PLAN B

Always have a Plan B. When you have your back against the wall, it usually means that your business model needs to be refined or needs a major overhaul. But it also means that you are likely to hit a cash crisis. That is the worst time to try to raise capital, and the process of fundraising can be so consuming that making the right improvements to your business model can be compromised. **That's why having a Plan B is essential, particularly during the highest risk points of business development, when you are rapidly expanding from the proof-of-concept stage. Or when a major new competitor enters the battlefield.** Plan B means you have a way to cut costs and preserve capital until you can get the business model on track. Having a practical Plan B is an essential and prudent insurance policy against risk.

Misconstrued risk wastes capital, energy, trust, and much else. Asking the right questions is a surprisingly relevant factor. As I have described, BlackBerry saw its business wander into substantial risk by failing to ask the questions centered on the real risks facing those businesses.

Hedge your bets intelligently. When reacting to adversity, don't make all of your adjustments in anticipation of a single scenario or to support a single sort of outcome. Predicting and planning against a single adverse scenario is a little like picking a lottery ticket winner in reverse. Try to influence a *range* of outcomes. Constantly gather intelligence, especially about the risks you can influence most. Foremost of these is the customer experience. Constantly learn from customers, retail clerks, and social media. Monitor negative comments and suggestions with intense attention.

One of the best ways to reduce risk is to talk directly to your consumers. The first level of feedback is the Net Promoter Score we discussed earlier. If your customer ratings are falling or if a competitor is moving ahead of you, these are flashing yellow lights warning you that danger is ahead. But there is no substitute to talking to your customers face-to-face or at least on the phone. This feedback is vital, both the good and the bad, during high-risk periods.

While there's no magic formula to eliminate risk, there are a lot of little things that you can do that can minimize risk. **For many effective business people, even a minimized range of risk is still outside their comfort zone. If risk remains a chronic, unsolvable problem for you personally, consider another seat on the bus. If you really aren't a risk taker, then you need to think twice about whether you're the right person to go out and try to build a billion-dollar business.** Or maybe you're not the person who should be taking the *biggest* risk. If you're less comfortable being out front as the risk taker, perhaps you should be sitting in another seat on the bus. That's not to say the role you occupy will be less important to the success of the enterprise. Great architects are not always great builders. Your contribution may still be essential to reducing risk for the whole team, because you're really good at something that's key to the success of the company.

Pivot zone mastery demands relentless preparation. Athletes train, train, train over and over to achieve just fractional improvements that can be the difference between winning and losing. It's the same for transformative company CEOs and teams. In the start-up game, preparation is indispensable.

Jim Breyer, ranked the No. 1 venture capitalist in the world several years in a row, routinely speaks about how important preparation is. As he told *Forbes*, success for his own firm Accel is reliant on keeping a "prepared mind."

I remember watching Steve Jobs prepare over and over, rehearsing every detail of his theatric product-introduction performances.

I've been told that Bill Maher, the television personality, still does a one-night-stand comedy routine in small towns just to hone his message and practice and practice. A 2012 piece on Jerry Seinfeld in *The New York Times* notes: "since 2000, Seinfeld has spent a portion of nearly every week doing stand-up. He is on track to do 89 shows this year, plus private appearances, which shakes out to about two performances a week."

The analogy to the entertainment world is not accidental. **Start-up entrepreneurs with aspirations of scaling big spend a massive amount of time pitching their concept in front of skeptical, often grim-faced investment analysts. You'd better learn to prepare both in running your business and in presenting your business.** But nowhere is the benefit of preparation most vital than when you have to execute a business pivot, especially in meeting an up-against-the-wall crisis.

Risk, failure, and rebounding are well recognized and deeply intertwined essentials in the entrepreneur's realm. Yet the governing dynamics are misunderstood in subtle but disabling ways:

- In trying to size up risk, many people, entrepreneurs included, do a poor job of distinguishing between the real and the imaginary.

- Instead of assuming risk-taking to be an exclusively inborn knack, we need to acknowledge the importance of experience, timing, intelligence-gathering, and outside mentoring in diminishing risk.

- **Entrepreneurs often postpone critical decisions hoping to gather "perfect information"—yet the very absence of perfect information is what makes moments transformative and opportunities disruptive. Seasoned entrepreneurs learn to advance sensibly with imperfect information.**

DEALING WITH FAILURE

In the high-risk world of business development, failure is an inevitable and continuous part of evolving a concept. If you view failure as essential to fine-tuning an idea, it's when and how you fail in the innovation cycle that become key measures of smart risk-taking.

Accidents happen in any high-risk enterprise—founding a business is no exception. When the failure rests clearly on your shoulders or on your watch, the setback can leave you devastated.

Failures can change the world—I know this firsthand.

MY BIG PUBLIC FAILURE: THE NEWTON

When Jim Cannavino, head of the IBM PC business, called me in December 1992 to congratulate us that the Mac had passed the IBM PC to become the largest-selling hardware PC in the world, we had only the briefest moment to enjoy the accomplishment. By then, thanks to Moore's Law, microprocessors were now powerful enough that a Windows-loaded PC armed with an Intel CPU from any of hundreds of manufacturers was able to run the same apps as the Mac just about as well. We badly needed a game changer to differentiate Apple from its competitors.

We had already made our big bet on a product code-named Newton. That development had begun several years earlier under the guidance of Apple's charismatic and talented head of Apple product development, Jean-Louis Gassée. He is the Apple executive who took over the Mac group after Steve Jobs left, and became a hero when his team developed and launched our very successful Macintosh II in 1987. Jean-Louis first assigned one of his favorite engineers, Steve Sakoman, to Newton. Jean-Louis later handed Newton off to one of our best engineer leaders, Larry Tesler, the same person who took Steve Jobs and Woz on their now famous tour of Xerox PARC. Larry recruited Steve Capps, one of the most respected original Mac software engineers, as lead software engineer on Newton in the Silicon Valley team and Ike Nassi, another brilliant engineer, to head up our team adjacent to MIT at One Kendall Square. One of our best product marketers, Michael Chao, headed Newton marketing. Putting such an impressive tech team on Newton shows how serious we were about the importance of PDAs.

The Newton was to be an entirely new direction for personal computing: A handheld personal digital assistant that would use artificial intelligence to do smart things, the Newton would ultimately be able to communicate with other PDAs wirelessly.

I named it a PDA (personal digital assistant) because we wanted the world to appreciate Newton as something very different from traditional knowledge worker tools that Apple, Microsoft, IBM, and Intel were so well known for. Newton wasn't a personal productivity tool. It was intended to be a very smart computerized assistant that utilized some first-generation artificial intelligence. It would be a miniaturized, handheld mobile device that people could carry around.

Four weeks before Newton's launch in June 1993, I got fired, and it caused me to take my eye off of Newton's final testing before it was released. Maybe, in different circumstances, I would have paid more attention and realized that Newton's handwriting recognition was still making many errors. There was no keyboard on a Newton, and the only way to enter information was to write on Newton's small screen with a pointing device. The launch was a failure. I had been Newton's biggest champion, and when the cartoonist Garry Trudeau made continual fun of Newton's ridiculously poor handwriting recognition, both Newton and I became objects of public ridicule. No excuses: I blew it with Newton.

THE NEWTON: NOT QUITE THE END OF THE STORY

Newton was launched in August 1993, a year before the Netscape Navigator browser and the World Wide Web. This was before there were many analog cellphones, way before the first digital mobile phone, and six years before Google or wireless data. Yet Newton pointed the right direction for the future.

Our Newton engineers needed a low-powered, floating-point microprocessor, but none existed until we met Hermann Hauser, a Cambridge University physicist and founder of the UK PC firm called Acorn. Hermann was creating an entirely new kind of microprocessor for mobile devices called ARM (for Acorn RISC Machine), and we teamed up with him to optimize the ARM processor for the graphic subroutines important to Newton. Apple ended up owning forty-three percent of ARM, and years later, in 1996, when Apple badly needed working capital to survive its near disastrous decision to license the Mac OS and to have the cash to acquire Steve Jobs' NeXT firm, Apple CEO Gil Amelio made the wise decision to sell Apple's stake in ARM for $800 million.

Over fifteen years later, ARM went on to be an incredibly successful $21 billion market cap public company, and its microprocessor has been used in about 29 billion mobile devices. The technology columnist Walt Mossberg, in his final *Wall Street Journal* contribution, cited Newton, the product that commercially failed, as the most important technology innovation in the twenty-two years he had covered high technology. I totally underestimated that successful smart mobile devices were almost fifteen years away, until Steve Jobs launched the iPhone in 2007.

When and how you fail in the innovation cycle become important lessons. What you want to do is learn how to fail fast and do your failing at the proof-of-concept stage, because it's a lot less expensive than at the expansion and execution-intensive stage. Serial entrepreneurs have an easier time raising capital because they have probably experienced extreme turbulence or even a near-death moment in their careers. Experiencing that and surviving is pretty awesome, and it also teaches you when to take your risks. One thing often said in Silicon Valley is: "Learn how to fail fast and, hopefully, cheap. If you're going to fail, do it in the lean way. Don't waste a lot of money failing, and, when you've failed, recognize it. Tuck away the best lessons you can from the setback and then move on and do something else." In Silicon Valley, you're schooled to accept failure as necessary, almost automatic. It's just part of fine-tuning. That attitude doesn't make you fearful or risk-shy. Just the opposite.

Here's what The North Face's cofounder Hap Klopp says about failure:

> *The first thing to get young companies comfortable with is the fact that they will make mistakes, and once they make those mistakes, it isn't the end of the world. Be able to gauge it, be able to mount it, to be able to limit the risk by limiting the amount of investment they're pursuing. That's the first thing.*
>
> *Fear is a precursor of failure. You've got to have the audacity that you truly can and will change the world. Let the world know that. Just over the hill, you will run into something you never anticipated. Unless you have*

the conviction that you'll whip that sort of challenge, you'll never survive the demanding road to success. You need sure-footed confidence to react to the unanticipated with resolve and decisiveness. That really makes the difference between a great leader and somebody who's merely a manager.

If you're going to be an entrepreneur, you have to expect that at some time, you are going to have a bad fall. It's inevitable, no matter how talented you are. You'll likely experience an occasion when you actually fail, and fail really big. Your natural instincts are to go and hide. Or hope that nobody heard about it. The reality is that you have to be willing to 'fess up and accept failure. Accept disappointment. Even accept humiliation. And you must be able to say, "I screwed up." A lot of people think I screwed up at some important moments. I can tell you from personal experience: It feels awful. When it happens, compel yourself to think about your failure in specific terms, not in broad generalities. When you do this, you can be far more constructive about the specific lessons you learn. It will also help you distinguish between the actual failures for which you may have been responsible and the generalized, but inaccurate blame others might conveniently try to assign to you.

WHY I GOT FIRED FROM APPLE

By 1993, I had been CEO of Apple for ten years. We had built the Mac to be the largest-selling personal computer in the world. We had $2 billion of cash in the bank, but we were under intense competition from Microsoft Windows and Intel's platform. There was a debate within Apple whether we should license our operating system. I was against it, because I believed it would lead us into a financial death spiral. What I didn't realize was that some of my executive team had lost confidence in me and went behind my back and convinced the Apple board that the board should fire me. I was ambushed and, under the pretext of a weak quarter in 1993, I was pushed out of Apple. I had no idea that I was going to be fired from the company.

History later validated how vulnerable Apple could quickly become by licensing its operating system, as the company subsequently burned through two CEOs in the following three years after I left, and the company nearly went bankrupt. When Steve Jobs came back to Apple, the first thing he did was to reverse the decision to license Mac's operating system.

Not long ago, I gave a speech before an audience of sixty very successful entrepreneurs who probably had earned between $100 million and $200 million each during their careers. Nothing registered more than my comments about the importance of failure. It was amazing how many of these very successful former executives came up to me afterward to talk about how meaningful their failures had been. All of them said their best judgments later in life stemmed from brutal and sometimes very embarrassing failures.

PERMISSION TO FAIL:
THE BIG AMERICAN ADVANTAGE

Imagine if you lived in another culture and failed; Germany for one. You're finished. Game over. Pick a new career, because failure is not accepted. And that's pretty true in most societies around the world. Failure is a black mark for life. South Korea, China, and Japan are countries that are educating a high level of technical talent, but their suicide rates rank among the world's top ten and are indicative of the devastating impact of failure and loss of face. What happens when failure isn't accepted? Many highly talented people refuse to take further risks.

Permission to fail is the Big American Advantage. Permission to fail is something that is still uniquely American. I was giving a speech in Mumbai, India, a few years ago, at their largest annual technology conference, called NASSCOM.

That's when it struck me how many Asian Indians had their success story unfold in America. That's one reason why there's a large immigration of highly trained and educated Indians to Silicon Valley. In fact, there isn't a Silicon Valley company that doesn't have, in its senior leadership, several Indians. India is known for its incredibly high-quality technical education with IIT, India Information Technology Institutes. What's the unique attraction of Silicon Valley? It's the learning experience and the permission to fail—without penalty; to just recycle the experience back into another opportunity. I can't stress this attitude enough.

Learning to pivot is a great tool, because at some point you are either going to have your back against the wall or indeed experience real failure. The key is to manage risk, always have a Plan B, and learn from your mistakes. Most of all, learn from your failures. They will prove to be the most precious teachers in your life.

8.

THE BEST ADVICE I CAN GIVE AN ENTREPRENEUR: FIND A MENTOR

A mentor is someone who allows you to see the higher part of yourself when sometimes it becomes hidden to your own view.
—Oprah Winfrey

The best advice I can give an entrepreneur? Find a mentor!

Why is it so important for an entrepreneur to have a mentor? When you're building a business, or repositioning your business, or changing the ground rules of a business, in many cases you're doing things where there's little precedent. Without precedents, you're compelled to make judgments and decisions about things where the facts are anything but perfect. If you don't have perfect facts, you're going to be relying on your instincts.

The billion-dollar businesses we're talking about developing will largely be the consequence of transformational moments, which—by their very nature—are periods of high risk. You probably had very little to do with creating the transformational moment that will have unlocked the opportunity. Odds are high that you'll have substantial domain expertise in just one area—and may have credible experience in a second—while a grasp of three or more domains might be in play in structuring the fledgling company.

Consider all the intangibles and uncertainties whirling around any new business that's truly innovative: You can be too early . . . you can be too late. Your first release of a product could be not good enough. And so on.

As a risk taker, if you want to limit risk, one of the best ways is to have another set of trusted eyes. The mentor's biggest role is to be just that. That's what the many executives I've mentored tell me is the most important help I can give a start-up CEO, and it's a role I am proud to perform. A mentor has to have some domain expertise that is going to be relevant to the person being mentored. Mentoring is not about pep talks. It's not about saying: "Go in there again and give it another try!" The heart of mentoring is helping a business founder or CEO with matters of judgment.

When I first began working at Apple, I often thought: "Gee, I wish I'd had a mentor." There weren't any around then. At least, I didn't know them when I was starting out. We didn't live in a world connected by email. We didn't have cellular phones. We didn't have the World Wide Web. Even through the 1980s, the idea that you could easily contact somebody who could give you a point of view on something just wasn't easy to do. Because communications were relatively far more difficult to maintain, mentor relationships among entrepreneurs—if they existed—were not common, and an individual was unlikely to have one beyond someone already in their immediate area.

Now we have all these communication and collaboration tools. People can supplement electronic communication with face-to-face meetings. It's much easier and faster to keep people in your network—especially a mentor—in touch and up to date with the latest information.

A mentor's influential role should never cloud or confuse decision-making. It's important that decisions are made within the company. If mentors are perceived as deciders, this has the potential to foster politics, and politics will lead to bad organizations. Politics are poison to a transformative company. There is such a thin line between success and failure.

Smart people still do dumb things, and mentors can be a big help in averting unnecessary stupidity.

Very smart companies, organizations, and leaders can and still do very dumb things. The symptoms of the stupidity can be incredibly transparent, in retrospect. The following list of head-scratching questions highlight some of the most dramatic dumb things done by major organizations in recent years:

• Why did Intel and Microsoft both miss the new era of mobility and cede the future to Apple and Google?

• Why did GM build the wrong next generation car—the Chevy Volt hybrid—and cede the electric car innovator role to Tesla?

• Why didn't the U.S. government convert its huge government truck fleets to much cheaper liquid natural gas fuel?

• Why didn't Health and Human Services properly customer test and design the technology to a scale that effectively supported the Affordable Care Act? This was President Obama's most important legislative program, and its implementers didn't properly anticipate that 30 million people would want to use this new form of insurance.

These are exactly the kind of mistakes mentors are well equipped to detect and avoid. Mentors can function as that valuable second pair of eyes and help identify major snafus in the making. Mentors can be so useful in spotting when leadership is focused on its own history-driven agenda, rather than framing issues with a customer-centered mindset. Many smart people are brilliant at competing or organizing but are tone-deaf at connecting the dots—especially in detecting and recognizing transformational moments.

They are unable to take the same facts and see entirely different possibilities.

Mentors can play a variety of roles: A skilled mentor can help reduce risks at moments of high turbulence. In addition to being another set of eyes, a skilled mentor can be:

- An advocate.
- A rainmaker who can sway influential opinion at key moments.
- A recruiter of talent.
- An adviser on raising capital.
- A check-and-balance observer of the CEO's style and performance, in a very nonthreatening way.

Mentors can supplement the role performed by a board of directors. As a mentor, the things that I focus on really fall outside of those traditional governance roles of boards. This doesn't mean that a board member cannot be a mentor, but it also doesn't mean that a mentor necessarily has to be a board member. A mentor, as I have said, helps the CEO maintain perspective during the most difficult moments and helps to anticipate them. Boards, on the other hand, tend to be involved in a more formal role, not a fluid and proactive one. Their oversight activities often include compensation, financial auditing, and policy resolutions. The board's obligations, perceived and real, often inhibit more relaxed and constructive mentoring relationships and guidance.

Mentoring must be built on a foundation of trust. A mentor can be effective only if the relationship between the mentor and the CEO is one of extremely high trust. In my case, I have a very simple first principle: I work only with people I like. Obviously, that functions in reciprocal terms too, and the person I'm mentoring has to like me as well. Why is that so important? Because you want to build a level of trust that supports sharing information back and forth from the mentor to the CEO, and the CEO to the mentor, as they deal with very tough things.

My focus is on those moments when a CEO might find themselves with their back against the wall and dealing with a situation, as I have said, that they may or may not have been part of creating. Nevertheless, they have to learn how to pivot. They have to make judgments. These judgments aren't always going to be popular in terms of their consequence or effect.

Most mentors need to have taken enough of a deep dive into the business that a CEO will not have to explain the business context to them each time a problem arises. The relationship should be close, intimate, and continuous enough to support regular contact and updating. Potential topics for discussion are those the CEO may not feel very comfortable talking about to anyone else directly in (or surrounding) the organization, including his or her board members. A mentor is not there to get any of the rewards of success in terms of recognition. The mentor is there, quietly in the background, as a resource for the CEO.

Mentors are not the only role models: There are also role models for mentors. Who is the best mentor role model I know? The answer is easy. His name is Bill Campbell. I recruited Bill Campbell to come to Apple in 1983 to become Apple's marketing and sales VP. Bill was working with Kodak at the time, but, more importantly, previously he had been coach of the Columbia University football team. Bill's coaching skills as a mentor are legendary in Silicon Valley. I brought Bill to Apple because our very young team needed a lot of coaching. Consider that the average age of the hundred people in Steve Jobs' Macintosh division at the time was twenty-two!

Bill went on after Apple to become CEO of Intuit and later its chairman. When Steve Jobs returned to Apple, Bill Campbell was one of his closest confidants, and Bill remains a long-serving Apple board member. He is best known as the mentor to Steve Jobs, Jeff Bezos, and Google's Larry Page and Eric Schmidt. Always in the background, never seeking a high public profile, Bill Campbell is by his very chemistry ideally suited to be a mentor role model. One knows that whatever they discuss with Bill remains private between him and them. He knows how to keep a secret. Bill has a superb sense of judgment and is the ultimate trusted pair of eyes for the best transformative company CEOs in the world. He's very emotional in a positive way and balances his intensity with a fine sense of humor. He never grandstands, and instills total trust with those he mentors, because it's never about Bill . . . it's always about them. He is completely honest, authentic, and totally trustworthy. Because he works in confidence, he can give tough love in a very private way. No one over the years has been more sought out for mentor advice or had more success at it than Bill Campbell. Bill recently retired from Apple's board after seventeen years as a director and more than thirty years of contributions to the company.

Mentors can help you spot perils that an entrepreneur engaged in the daily business can overlook or minimize. Mentors can ask provocative questions like:

- Are we taking too much risk?
- Have we overextended ourselves?
- Are we running too low on cash?

Without doubt, a mentor can help your confidence when it needs to be bolstered. A mentor can also get you to wake up when danger looms by saying, "Hey, you need to take this situation more seriously." A mentor will at least allow you to balance your instincts against the mentor's point of view— whether you are a founder, a start-up CEO, or an executive in an existing business who is dedicated to being an adaptive innovator.

Mentors don't make tipping-point decisions, but they can make an incalculable difference when tipping-point decisions must be made. If you've been a mentor, as I have been for decades, you've made a lot of mistakes. You learn from that. You've had some successes. You've learned something from that. Your value isn't that you come in and run these businesses—mentors don't run businesses. As I said, they don't do just pep talks. They are able to come in and give a context and often can offer a point of view on judgment issues that the CEO has to make.

For six years, I have been mentoring John Duffy, CEO and cofounder of 3C Interactive, a dynamic mobile services company. Duff has been diligent at recognizing when to recruit new talent and train his current managers with new skills. He has gotten so good at it that it has actually helped me with some of my other businesses. The skills a team needs at proof-of-concept are very different than your team needs at the expansion stage. If you can't scale, you won't have a valuable firm.

Mentors can be particularly helpful to promising companies in comeback situations. Here's an example from my own direct experience with a company I mentioned earlier. Audax Health is a health social networking and gamification company. Audax's founder and CEO, Grant Verstandig, is twenty-five years old. Although we are from different generations, we have become close friends as I have been mentoring him for the past two years. Audax's first product release was a bomb. He didn't let that failure overcome him. He quickly recovered by recruiting a stronger team and learning lessons from what didn't work the first time. Grant's first product development team was in their twenties, and their first prototype was a disappointment. It seemed aimed at a person in their twenties, not the prime consumer in mind, whom we targeted as a forty-year-old woman. After his early failure, Grant regrouped, recruiting a much more experienced product team, and Grant personally led the product development. The results that followed have been spectacular.

What is Grant creating? A web destination that fills a multifaceted void in health care. Grant and his team looked at the web and concluded that no available aggregate destination gives you "the engagement and connectivity of

Facebook, the retention or the enjoyment of a Zynga game, or the recommendation engine of Amazon." Audax was recently acquired for a sizable sum by the health care giant Optum.

MY BEST ADVICE TO BABY BOOMERS

Become a mentor!

Many in the retiring baby boomer generation can look forward to a long, healthy life. These accomplished and experienced leaders should be asking themselves, "Why shouldn't I become a mentor?" I see some of my contemporaries bored after luxuriating in lots of golf and travel during their retirement years.

Your brain atrophies unless it's exercised and challenged. You can't sit it out on the sidelines for many years in retirement and then expect to be quickly back at the top of your game. Consider mentoring: The sooner, the better, particularly if it's in your domain of expertise.

So while this book is based on what I've learned in a lifetime in business and the strategies that adaptive innovators and adaptive corporations might use to build transformative new businesses, my best advice I can give an entrepreneur is this: **Find a mentor!** Have you already enjoyed a meaningful business career and do you want to help guide the destiny of business events as we enter the greatest period of entrepreneurial opportunity the world has ever known? **Then establish bonds with worthy younger executives, and be a mentor!**

PART V

MOONSHOT: A SUMMARY AND CONCLUDING REMARKS

*There is only one boss. The customer. And he can fire
everybody in the company from the Chairman on down,
simply by spending his money somewhere else.*
—Sam Walton, founder,
Walmart and Sam's Club

Today's Moonshot—the computer as an automated intelligent assistant propelling the customer to be in control—has already happened. It has enabled transformative
entrepreneurs to build successful, disruptive businesses
centered totally on the customer. This book, *Moonshot!*, is
about how to build successful, transformative businesses
centered totally on the customer. It's about why this is the
best time in history to build these businesses—because
the convergence of amazing technologies like cloud computing and sensors are enabling radical changes to traditional business processes, which will allow for completely
disruptive pricing. And it's about the addition of two other
incredible technologies, Big Data and mobile devices, like
smartphones, which are fundamentally shifting the power
from producers-in-control to customers-in-control.

The combination of these four exponential technologies
are growing so fast they are creating a network effect. The

result: People around the world—hundreds of millions of them—can be connected in real time. There has never been anything like it in history. This transformative moment is the Moonshot that I introduced at the beginning of the book. It is the shifting of economic power from business producers to smarter customers. This transformation is enabled by these four amazing digital technologies, each of which is growing at an exponential rate. They are very smart, personalized systems that in profound ways will change every industry in the world. Two of these technologies, cloud computing and mobile devices, are already touching billions of users. Soon, tens of billions of miniature wireless sensors will produce gigantic masses of interrelated data. This data will be subjected to a new generation of mathematical algorithms in data science incorporating artificially intelligent systems that will analyze consumer behavior right down to the individual person and automatically predict outcomes, helping all of us to make better informed decisions. This Moonshot enables the power shift toward much smarter customers.

Those companies and entrepreneurs that can adapt will be the big winners. These transformative businesses will be built by a new breed of entrepreneurs I call "adaptive innovators." They are already building today and will continue to create truly remarkable new businesses in the future. Adaptive innovators must also lead existing companies to become "adaptive corporations"—the survivors and indeed the winners in their industries.

Ultimate control of all of these new, transformative companies will be with the customer. Consumers have complete access today to information unheard of a few years ago. This includes where to find the best price, how products and services are rated by users, and what their friends recommend. And they can buy instantly with the click of a smartphone. The richness of this information will continue to grow exponentially in the future. It's almost unimaginable how fast this will happen and the power it will give the customer.

Those companies that create customer experiences

never dreamed of before—like immediate access to convenient, affordable health care, for example—will become huge successes. And those companies that choose not to adapt are likely to be disrupted and may not survive. I have been building businesses all my life—it's what I do and what I love. Yes, it entails risk. Yes, there are ups and downs. And, yes, along the way, you're likely to find your back against the wall. But there has never been a better time to build.

WHAT ADAPTIVE INNOVATORS NEED TO KNOW

When I joined Apple in 1983, the term "knowledge worker" wasn't yet in the popular lexicon. Apple had been running a print ad with a headline pointing out all the things you could do with a personal computer. Back then, the personal computer was a curiosity. Only a few thought of it as a useful tool for the mind. Only a few years later, PCs and Macs became indispensable personal productivity machines for knowledge workers.

These are early days for adaptive innovators. Of course, many people have been adapting and innovating for some time, but "adaptive innovator" isn't a recognizable term yet like Clayton Christensen's "disruptive innovation." If that's true, why even coin the term "adaptive innovator"? For one simple reason: *focus*. If one is going to be really good at something, you need to know what it is you intend to be really good at, and you need to focus. The following points have all been discussed in this book. Absorbing them and making them a permanent part of your mindset will help you be successful:

1) **Be curious.** Be an optimist. Adaptive innovators are inspired by what's *possible*, but focused on what's *probable*. Entrepreneurs aren't just dreamers, they are doers. My brothers, Arthur and David, and I wake up early every day re-energized and optimistic, curious about the world around us, but always focused on getting good

stuff done. These are traits from childhood that we share in common, but these are actually learned behaviors, and that means you can learn them, too.

2) **Unpack ideas.** We all tend to use jargon, but transforming an idea demands that you go well beyond the jargon to the clear, fundamental meaning beneath. Ideas are powerful. Unpacking one is about taking deep dives into an idea; twisting and turning it to see an idea in different ways. The deeper your dive into an idea, the more creative will be your insights. Unpacking an idea may sound counterintuitive at first, as in Steve Jobs' process on zooming out to connect the dots and then zooming in to simplify. Unpacking an idea takes intense focus. As I read about things every day, I keep asking myself: "Is there something here that might apply to the idea I'm trying to unpack?" Ideas without context are just a commodity. It's usually a surprise to the really smart young class valedictorians that when they arrive in Silicon Valley they soon realize that being smart is nothing special, and that good ideas are simply pretty common. Everyone is smart in Silicon Valley and good ideas in such places are routine. So what is a smart person with good ideas to do? Learn to develop context for your good ideas so they may actually become valuable. Context comes from experience. Trying and failing is a building-block experience to get context. Teaming with other smart people who have different domain expertise is another way to get context. These are the kinds of immersions you need to truly unpack an idea and unleash its power.

3) **Learn in layers.** Thinking visually can help. For me, the best learning is like peeling the layers of an onion, except in reverse. Instead of peeling off layers, I add new layers of learning and information every day. Typically a new bit of learning may just be something that sparks my curiosity. It's why I always keep a notebook with

me so I can jot down a key word or a reference I want to check later or an insight I learned from someone in a conversation. Never be afraid to borrow a good idea as long as you give attribution to the source.

4) **There has to be a better way, and never ever give up in finding it.** Steve Jobs was never satisfied. He kept pushing himself and everyone around him. Steve kept raising the bar. He would repeat the mantra, reminding us that repetition doesn't destroy the prayer. This mantra actually came from the talented and charismatic Jean-Louis Gassée, who headed Macintosh product development after Steve Jobs left and created the successful Mac II. Embracing the doctrine *"There has to be a better way"* is an exhausting experience. Some quit. The best stay with it. At Apple, when a product actually shipped, against unimaginable timelines, even the most talented and skeptical on the team were amazed at and empowered by what they had accomplished.

5) **Prepare!** The best athletes are naturally gifted, but even they train constantly and invest hours of practice *every day*. It's no different for the best adaptive innovators. What do I practice every day? Examining systems, for one. I try to understand everyday products and services around me as systems. Why do we do something in a particular way? Many conventional systems that we take for granted were created almost by mere chance or are legacies of a random event that led to a success years earlier. In other words, there are now accepted ways of doing things because that's just how things happened to evolve.

The deeper one explores why things are the way they are, the more often you will discover that random events are at the root of universally accepted practices. You will also find that powerful incumbents aren't quite as powerful as they may at first appear. Challengers actually may have better odds at success than they might consider. So keep preparing yourself to get better and better at whatever you do. Get really good at something, and you don't have to be good at everything. You want to be as well prepared for your journey as you can be.

The most formidable tools of the adaptive innovator are very smart, highly personalized data systems that can help you deploy resources to realize your vision. You don't necessarily need to understand the details of the engineering and algorithms behind the systems any more than you need to master how electricity is generated or water is pumped by public utility services. Instead, you do need to know how to use adaptive innovator tools, just as knowledge workers had to learn how to use personal productivity tools.

6) **Put the Customer at the Center of Your Business Concept.** As you consider a really transformative business concept, it should leverage your domain expertise and create a customer experience never realized before in that industry. Couple this with automated processes that utilize the exponential technologies we have been talking about in this book, and you can offer a disruptive price that can rapidly gain market share against even the most established companies or brands.

WHAT ADAPTIVE CORPORATIONS NEED TO KNOW

TEN FIRST PRINCIPLES FOR THE ADAPTIVE CORPORATION

Moonshot! is about lessons learned over a lifetime, through both mistakes and successes. It's grounded on ten key principles that I believe are essential to the building of transformative businesses.

These principles apply if you are an entrepreneur creating a new company and are *critical* if you are an adaptive innovator inside an existing business intent on reviving an established company. There is no shortcut to the hard work involved in applying them:

1) **Adaptive corporations flourish in industries poised for change.** Innovation begins at the edge of an industry when a different domain expertise converges and collides with an established industry domain. A decade ago only a few select industries were poised for fundamental redefinition. Today, nearly every industry is a candidate for transformation because of the exponential growth in digital technology. Smarter, better informed customers multiply their influence impact through the network effect.

- When I was at Pepsi-Cola Company, it took us fifteen years to build Mountain Dew into a highly successful big brand. Xiaomi is a Chinese mobile device company founded in 2010. It sold more than 7 million phones in 2012, more than 18 million phones in 2013, and is projected to sell an estimated 60 million mobile devices in 2014. In fact, in just four years of existence, the company has achieved a market valuation of over $10 billion.

- The taxi industry itself may not have been a growth industry, yet Uber has created one of the most valuable growth companies by delivering a better way that customers love.

- Renting out one's home to travelers wasn't even deemed an industry until Airbnb created a better way of serving customers than traditional hotels by organizing people who were willing to share spare rooms in their homes and offer lodging at disruptive prices.

- The list of industries undergoing comparable change is virtually endless.

2) **Survival is driven by adaptation.** Charles Darwin emphasized adaptability as essential to evolution. In a Churchill Club interview recently, Reid Hoffman maintained that Silicon Valley recognized that scale, not cash flow, was the most important measure of business promise. Use scale as a reflection of the network effect and measures like the Net Promoter Score as evidence that the customer experience is positively accepted.

3) **Zero in on the most challenging customer problems in your industry that need really big solutions.** Focus on the possible, not the probable. Then imagine what a 10× better customer solution might be, even if you think it's not practical today. Don't worry if your 10× idea seems impractical; stretch your imagination, knowing it's OK to be wrong. Attack opportunity expansively. If you don't do it, someone else will.

4) **Learn how to exploit failure.** Thomas Edison said he had to discover 10,000 materials that didn't work as a light bulb filament before he found the one that did. Failure is fundamental to creativity. Fortunately, permission to fail is baked into our culture in the U.S., while it is alien to many societies.

5) **The most successful adaptive corporations are obsessed with continually creating exceptional customer experiences.** No compromises. Consequently, the most important metrics will always be customer metrics. Businesses dedicated to high gross margins flourished only when producers were in control. Brands are built today by smarter consumers in a customer-in-control world. Today's technologies make the data you'll need easily and affordably accessible. Get rid of the traditional, long-winded business plan. Initiate the customer plan and use Back From the Future Planning.

6) **Regard your business as an end-to-end system tailored around a continuous feedback loop beginning with creating the best possible customer experience.** Cycle customer input into your decision-making in real time. As Jeff Bezos said in the early days of Amazon, "The right frame of mind is that your customers are loyal to you, right up until the moment somebody else offers them better service."

7) **Put the right people on the bus.** And make sure they are in the right seats. Never make staffing choices that shortchange the customer experience, and use Back From the Future Planning to anticipate when you will need to have people in place to grow the business.

8) **Transformative businesses are never successfully run by consensus; there has to be a clear decider.** New companies have an important advantage over established businesses because the decider is usually the founder and CEO. If the CEO is the decider of systemic design, then the company will need talented adaptive innovators to help build the dream and adapt the business as challenges and new opportunities arise. Adaptive corporations are the antithesis of rigid organizations, steeped in legacy policies and protocols. Corporations trying to adapt should keep in mind an observation made by Peter Drucker: "The bottleneck is always at the top of the bottle."

9) **Exploit the real-world context in which you are operating.** Change is happening faster than ever:

- Two-thirds of Apple's revenue comes from products it released after 2007.
- In 1999, 38 million people had broadband. Today 1.2 billion have it on their mobile phones!
- The world's middle class is growing by the billions,

especially in emerging markets, where frugal expenses and resourcefulness are creating cheaper, faster, better product and service alternatives. Leverage today's unprecedented availability of low-cost capital to fuel expansion.

10) **Be perpetually governed by the principle that there has to be a better way.** Never allow yourself to become complacent. Today, it's appalling that seventy-four percent of businesses don't have a plan to stay competitive in the new mobile world. Recognize that the bar is continually moving higher. Only through relentless discipline and focused curiosity will you have the stamina and agility to pivot and adjust to the changes the future will inevitably bring.

LOOKING OUT A FEW YEARS

I have been building businesses all my life, and I can honestly say this is the most exciting time ever to be part of the business world. Technology is changing so quickly, it's making it affordable and easy for entrepreneurs to build great companies much faster than ever before. Smarter manufacturing in automated factories, the expansive presence of automated warehouses, and ordering an unlimited selection of products online are a familiar part of our early twenty-first century world.

By the early 2020s, automation won't just automate existing processes and take instructions from humans; automated systems will themselves be "intelligent" and able to do things seemingly on their own. What will allow this to happen? Sensors—maybe 30 billion to 50 billion of them—will be everywhere, and they will be connected to some sort of system. The boundaries between the online and offline world will disappear. Sensors will know *where* we are and will have the artificial intelligence to accurately predict our likely wants, needs, and discretionary spending habits.

Sensors will communicate machine-to-machine, creating highly personalized data about each of us in real time and storing this data in the cloud. Mobile payments will be far more advanced than just enabling a user to pay with a smartphone. Mobile payments will use end-to-end automated intelligent systems, be smart enough to build an audit trail record of everything you spend, and automatically make informed decisions for you that will enhance your credit score and qualify you automatically for special offers and electronic coupons.

Also by the early 2020s, customers will have increased information transparency that will change traditional brand marketing and how brands are valued. Customers will more likely trust their smart systems more than many of the brands they trust most today. Futurist Gerd Leonhard, CEO of the Future Agency, observed, "Machines will know us better than our closest friends." By the early 2020s, customers will be the winners, with many more affordable alternatives. This trend bodes well for a more affordable middle-class experience.

In fact, at this moment, high-tech companies are very focused on the new era of automated intelligent systems. IBM has created Watson, for example, an automated system that processes information more like a human than a computer by understanding natural language, generating hypotheses based on evidence, and learning as it goes. And Microsoft has created Cortana, an artificial intelligent agent. I believe Microsoft's new CEO, Satya Nadella, is envisioning a world in which these kinds of virtual assistants are smart enough to function as real-life human assistants might.

A FINAL WORD

*The future belongs to those who see possibilities
before they become obvious.*
                              —John Sculley

Sony, Sears, Motorola, and Kodak were great twentieth-century brands that earned customers' trust back when producers were in control. A trusting relationship has always been the hallmark of a great brand. It used to be that building a reputation took lots of time and money. Warren Buffet said, "It takes twenty years to build a reputation and five minutes to ruin it." Today, brands can be built much more quickly, but they can still perish in a flash.

What do such ascendant new brands as Airbnb, Uber, and Xiaomi have in common? They are brands built by smarter customers, not by large companies with big spending budgets. Customer trust in these new transformative businesses is based on consumers sharing their experiences with other consumers. It's all about scale. The network effect promotes awareness of cheaper, faster, better, and more convenient alternatives to hotels, taxis, and inexpensive high-quality mobile devices. The customer data supporting these powerful business concepts is a more authentic way to create demand than clever advertising slogans. Smart data will drive a new generation of "exceptional customer experience brands."

Smart data can also drive the systemic design of a better way disruptive workflow. My wife, Diane, and I were having lunch recently at Hong Kong's Peninsula Hotel with Liam Casey, one of Ireland's most successful entrepreneurs and known *in China* as "Mr. China." I first met Liam a decade ago when his supply-chain contract manufacturing business, PCH International, was making accessories for mobile devices like the iPod and Microsoft's Zune. In those days PCH was not well known and its revenues were still small. Today, PCH transacts several billions of dollars of revenue annually and Liam Casey is a strategic vendor partner with Apple, Beats, and retailers like Radio Shack. What's so impressive about Liam's better end-to-end system is he has no warehouses and requires no inventory in the channel. PCH revolutionized the consumer electronics industry—especially in its delivery system for personalized iPod cases—and has disrupted end-to-end distribution costs enough to offset the air freight expense.

Earlier I mentioned the Chinese mobile-device maker Xiaomi and how they sold 100,000 smartphones over the Internet in China in just ninety seconds in one campaign. If brand trust is being built by well-informed customers getting personalized comparative shopping data with referrals on which products other customers rate as best, and if they also can expect disruptive flash sales prices too, then how can a traditional consumer electronics giant like Sony with substantial overhead, R&D expense, and thousands of products compete? The answer: Not easily.

In the 1980s, Steve Jobs and I used to visit Akio Morita, Sony cofounder and the visionary who created the Sony Walkman. Sony was the Apple of that era, and it stood out from all the other consumer electronics firms of that day with its innovative, beautifully designed, premium-quality products. If Sony could become vulnerable to disruption, what other highly respected companies today are at risk to new transformative alternatives?

One of the most inspiring visions of the future is told by Lisa Gansky, in her book *The Mesh: Why the Future of Business Is Sharing*. Her insights are brilliant and I encourage you to read her book. One of her most perceptive assertions is: "The mesh economy is where people share talents, goods, and services that leads to new communities-of-interest, new organizations, and new business models."

In the beginning of *Moonshot!*, I described how the Millennial generation is different. Its members are very comfortable with sharing and renting. They don't keep score the way my generation has done by what we own. This transformation is not only refreshing. It may also give some clues as to how an affordable and adaptable middle-class economy will function in the future, especially as some traditional jobs will be replaced by automated systems.

According to Mort Zuckerman's insightful OpEd essay in *The Wall Street Journal* in July 2014, there are 28 million part-time workers in the U.S. "Only 47.7% of adults in the U.S. are working full time," the essay notes. The millions of part-time workers have been decoupled for whatever reasons from full-time employment with one employer. This is an early indicator that people will need to create their own jobs, because there won't be enough companies or other organizations hiring as many people who need jobs. Necessity is the mother of invention. People will need to be resourceful, and this will lead many to become independent contractors or entrepreneurs.

The sharing economy, described by Lisa Gansky, isn't just about sharing your home or car with someone else or renting a dress from the very successful retailer Rent the Runway. The sharing economy will also be about sharing a job, or bidding for skilled project work with online services like eLance, or for physical work from a service like TaskRabbit. Other examples of people getting into business for themselves are Etsy in the arts-and-crafts domain or Feastly for people opening their homes for a dinner they prepare for paying guests. In 2001, as I have noted, author Daniel Pink coined the term "Free Agent Nation," and today it's obvious that his vision was prescient.

The Moonshot has happened. We are all getting smarter because smarter data is making all of us smarter customers. Adaptive innovators who seize this moment will never have a better time than now to create a billion-dollar transformative business. Others may not create a new innovative company, but will share in the adaptation to this new world of smarter customers. New business models will engage them in new forms of employment, offering new ways to utilize one's talents, and adapting to new ways of sharing products and services.

You can either worry about the future or you can be inspired by its opportunities. The choice is yours. What I am confident about is that the changes ahead will be as different from the future as the world today is from the incredibly simple life of my childhood in Bermuda. Be curious and be inspired. Take some risk. Life is a journey, and even with some failures I've had along the way, I know I wouldn't want to have missed any of it.

Writing this book has given me the opportunity to reflect on what an amazing time this is to be in business. I hope that by sharing some of my observations and insights, a new generation of adaptive innovators, inside and outside of today's corporations, will be inspired to build their own hugely successful transformative businesses and to find their own better way to make those differences that will indeed change the world.

AFTERWORD I

MY BROTHER JOHN

When I first approached my brother John about writing a book, he had absolutely no interest. He'd already written a book, he said—*Odyssey: Pepsi to Apple*, twenty-five years ago—and was today much more interested in mentoring entrepreneurs than writing the typical "trophy book" chronicling a business leader's successes.

In fact, he continued, "I actually learned a lot more from my failures than from my successes." That got me thinking. So I asked him, "Then why not write about your failures? And while you're at it, why not tell the world what both your successes and failures have taught you about how to build a business?" I watched John, as I have for all of my life, knowing the look he gets when the wheels start turning. I had his attention. Later, we started talking about how to build transformative businesses using today's remarkable exponentially expanding technologies. He said that what's really happening today in the new world of cloud computing, sensors, Big Data, and mobile devices is enabling an incredible "Moonshot"—the effect of which is an unprecedented power shift from producers to customers-in-control. When he realized this Moonshot could change everything, he was all in.

What most people don't realize is that John Sculley has been a builder all his life. During our childhood in Long Island and Bermuda, John was fascinated with electronics, particularly radios and TVs. He spent hours reading *Popular Science* and *Popular Mechanics* interspersed with taking apart and rewiring radios. He was an avid ham radio operator, and in 1953, at fourteen, built a color television long before color TV became mainstream. He also built a remote TV tuner that allowed him to change stations—although at that time he had only three channels to choose between—from the comfort of his bed.

During his sixteen years at Pepsi, John's happiest times were spent on an entrepreneurial journey that eventually made him CEO. His favorite assignment was starting PepsiCo International Foods, where he built and acquired snack foods businesses around the world. It is today a huge PepsiCo business unit. John had mixed feelings about later being promoted to president and CEO of Pepsi-Cola Company in the U.S., but focused his efforts on innovations aimed at building Pepsi and Mountain Dew into megabrands.

As we all know, John's most visible business role was at Apple, where he spent a decade as CEO. Again, he was happiest as a builder, taking the breakthrough Macintosh computer that Steve Jobs and Steve Wozniak had created and growing it into the best-selling personal computer in the world. When John was fired by Apple in 1993, he made the mistake of jumping into the first job offered to him on the rebound. Soon after, he hit rock bottom. He exited big business, lowered his profile, and decided to start again by mentoring aspiring entrepreneurs and incubating promising start-ups—reconnecting with his roots as a builder. As all who have worked with him know, this has truly been his life's greatest work.

Since then, for more than twenty years, John has been building and investing in rapidly growing companies across many markets. These range from consumer to technology to health care in the U.S. and all around the globe.

While John Sculley has had many successes as a CEO, his first love has always been building rather than managing or governing. And as a mentor and entrepreneur, he is truly exceptional. He blends the perspective from running large global corporations with the cutting-edge know-how he has gained from his more recent successes. That wisdom shines when he coaches CEOs, speaks to global audiences, or shares advice on the pages of this book. At moments of decision, challenge, or reinvention, John's impact is unparalleled. Fueled by decades of hands-on business leadership and a lifetime of creative thinking, John is at his best when challenging assumptions, leading colleagues into their "pivot zone," or facing up-against-the-wall moments where everything depends on what happens next.

Today, John works passionately seven days a week, fueled by his vision for what is possible and the role business plays in changing the world. He sees the coming wave of disruption as both a necessity for global economic well-being and an incredible opportunity for business leaders of all types. Schooled, literally, by unique successes, failures, and hands-on experiences, John loves to share his most important lessons from a lifetime of high-impact business leadership.

In addition to the material in this book, John has developed a compelling online video series, "How to Build a Successful Business," that dives deep into important themes of business building and innovation. His candid and enlightening coaching, as well as his interviews with great entrepreneurs like Apple cofounder Steve Wozniak, Dr. Mehmet Oz—America's best-known physician—and Wolfgang Puck, one of America's leading chefs, go beyond the lessons you'd learn at college or in business school. With groundbreaking candor and world-class success stories, his interviews— found at **JohnSculley.com**—give today's business builders the "up close and personal" examples they need to create the winning businesses of tomorrow.

As John reflects on the biggest problems facing the world today, the jobs crisis is clearly at or near the top of the list. Without jobs, there is no hope and no future. The only way to create sustainable jobs, in John's view, is to build new businesses. This is what John Sculley is all about. The insatiable curiosity that John exhibited in his childhood burns just as bright today. While John continues to build during every waking hour of every day, he has chosen to share his experiences with the world, and this is an enormous privilege for all of us.

—David Sculley
September 2014

AFTERWORD II

FATHER AND GRANDFATHER—
TWO MAJOR INFLUENCES

Our father, Jack, and our Bermudian grandfather, W.B. Smith, had significant influence on our lives. Our mother, W.B.'s daughter Margaret, a horticulturalist and artist, created a loving, welcoming family home life. Dad had earned a summa cum laude degree in the Classics at Princeton University in 1932 and then went on to Columbia Law School. Because of the Depression, he had to put himself through law school; he subsequently spent his career as a New York lawyer. He commuted nearly five arduous hours a day by train from our home in St. James, Long Island. At the same time, he was committed to local civic affairs in Long Island where he was our village mayor, chairman of St. Johnland's, a retirement home, and on the boards of the local library and hospital. Dad gave us guidance, but never really pushed us. Rather, he led by example, and we learned the importance of a good education, hard work, thoughtfulness, and integrity. He also became an important father figure for several of our cousins.

Although we did not realize it until he died suddenly of a stroke, while we were still in school, he had for years been under severe financial pressure in order to provide for our excellent educations. As we look back, we realize that perhaps the most important thing we learned from our father was perseverance: never, ever to give up, even when the wind is in your face. That lesson has helped my brothers and me on a number of important occasions. We remember the sacrifices Dad made for us and are always grateful.

Dad and W.B. were very close and enjoyed many laughs together, particularly during our summers in Bermuda, but they were complete opposites professionally. While Dad was a lawyer, W.B. was a Bermudian marine engineer, an entrepreneur, and a Member of the Bermudian Parliament. He started his working life by getting fired, at the age of fifteen, in 1890 from his parents' local department store, H.A. & E. Smith's on Front Street in Hamilton, Bermuda. Then he hopped on a freighter bound for Liverpool, England. He worked there as a boilerman's apprentice at the Cammell Laird Shipyard for five years. Liverpool at that time was the shipping center of the world, while the Industrial Revolution in Northern England was at its height. W.B. was fascinated by the emerging steam engine technology and equipment. After a short stay in Bermuda, he and his new wife, Mabel, moved to Elizabeth, New Jersey, for a few years. He worked for the marine architect John P. Holland on the first working submarine sold to the U.S. Navy, the USS *Holland*. It became the prototype for the Royal Navy's Holland Class submarines. Upon return to Bermuda, W.B. set up a marine engineering company and built a lighthouse and a bridge, and repaired numerous ships passing through Bermuda. His entrepreneurial skills led him to ship bunkering and water catchment, and he captained his own freight schooner in the Caribbean during World War II. Additionally, he helped our Aunt Madeline build a local perfume factory and popular tourist attraction, the Bermuda Perfumery. Until W.B. died, at the age of 94, he worked nearly every day of his life.

What made W.B. such an interesting entrepreneur was

his insatiable curiosity. He didn't care what others thought: He followed his interests and pursued them with passion. I think my brothers and I realize the important gift of curiosity we inherited from our grandfather that guides us constantly. What we also remember with great fondness were the stories of his colorful life that he would entertain us with during summer evenings in Bermuda. Like our father, W.B. made a significant impact on our lives in so many ways.

—Arthur Sculley
September 2014

THE SCULLEY BROTHERS

From left to right: Arthur Sculley, former head of J.P. Morgan's Private Bank; John Sculley, former CEO of Pepsi Cola U.S. and Apple; and David Sculley, former CEO of H.J. Heinz USA.

ACKNOWLEDGMENTS

A number of people helped me with *Moonshot!* and this book never would have happened without them. I am deeply grateful to each and every one. This starts with my brother David, who had the original concept, works with me every day, and has been the indispensable quarterback of the team. This also includes Ron Beyma, an experienced, gifted business writer who grasped my voice from the start and helped achieve an ambitious timetable by combining a tireless work ethic with a collaborative, team-oriented style. And special thanks goes to Brad Mooberry, who not only designed the cover, but also provided content and fact checking on a daily basis with amazing perception and dedication.

My sincere gratitude also goes to my brother Arthur, who provided a unique, in-depth understanding of emerging markets. To our publisher, RosettaBooks, and their able team led by Arthur Klebanoff, and particularly to Hannah

Bennett, their unflappable production manager who guided this book to market. To Steve Cody and his Peppercomm public relations group for their insights and support. To Ellen Leanse for her advice and valuable introductions to some very successful entrepreneurs. To Merrill Perlman for her experienced, professional line editing. To Misha Beletsky for his thoughtful and creative graphic design. To Barry Yarkoni for managing administrative details, including invaluable transcriptions of our extensive interviews. To our transcribers, Danae Anderson and Sarah Lopes. To Adam MacDonald, our talented executive producer, and his team, including Chris Turnow, our executive director, and Valerie Thomas, our film editor. And to the incredible group of some of the world's best entrepreneurs whom I had the privilege of interviewing on video. This included Woz (Steve Wozniak), Dr. Mehmet Oz, Wolfgang Puck, Leslie Blodgett, Tim Gannon, Julia Hartz, Julie Wainwright, Hap Klopp, Randy Parker, Steve Perlman, Doug Menuez (and a special thank you for the wonderful photos), David Steinberg, Grant Verstandig, Dennis Ratner, Dan Gittleman, Martin Varsavsky, Doug Solomon, and my son Jack Sculley.

I would like to conclude by recognizing my wife, Diane. She is not only my inspiration, but my constant sounding board and partner. Her tireless research for *Moonshot!* was critical. More importantly, she has given me the encouragement and support I needed to make this the best, most productive time in my life. I've never been happier or healthier.

—John Sculley
September 2014

INDEX

Bare Escentuals 158
bareMinerals 158
Basham, Bob 110
Bayesian statistics 15
Beatles 129
Beats 193
Bentonville (Arkansas) 78
Bermuda 195
Berners-Lee, Tim 86
"better way" and "There has to be
    a better way" xii–xiii, 21, 47,
    76, 77, 80, 83–91, 95, 99, 134,
    147, 149, 159, 185, 187, 190, 193,
    195
Beverly Hills, (California) 84, 110
Bezos, Jeff x, 24, 28, 36, 40, 92–95,
    100, 149, 174, 189
Bhusri, Aneel 89
"bicycles for the mind" 10
Big American Advantage, The
    168–69
Big Data ix, 15, 38, 58, 76, 93, 135,
    148, 150, 155, 156, 181
Bilbao (Spain) 19
Bill and Melinda Gates Founda-
    tion 35
billion-dollar business(es) and
    concept(s) x, xii, xv, xvi,
    38–48, 75–116, 124, 129–30, 135,
    142, 143, 144, 147, 150, 157, 161,
    170, 195
BJP Party 66
BlackBerry 97–98, 126–28, 161
BlackBerry Bold 126–27
Blecharczyk, Nathan 85, 140
Blodgett, Leslie 158
Bloom, Allan 51
Bloomberg Businessweek 65
Bloomberg, Mayor Michael x
Bloomberg Surveillance 123
"Bloomin' Onion" (Outback Steak-
    house) 110
Blumenthal, Neil 96
BMW 101–2
Bock, Laszlo 141
Bollywood 67
Borders 40
Branson, Richard x, 102–3
Brazil 64, 72
Breyer, Jim 162
Brioni xiv

broadband 189
Brown University 44, 88
Bryant, Adam 141
Bryant, Kobe 119–20, 135
Buffett, Warren 192
Buick (General Motors) 71
bundled services 67
Business Insider 64, 72, 123
business plan xii–xiii, 150–52, 153,
    188
Business-to-Business (B2B) 25,
    89–91, 152
BYOD (bring your own device)
    127, 157
Byte Shop 9

Cahill, Satjiv 18
CalTech 32
Cambridge (Massachusetts) 43
Cambridge University 165
Camp, Garrett 85
Campbell, Bill 174–75
Canada 54
Cannavino, Jim 163
Capps, Steve 164
*Capturing the World's Emerging
    Middle Class* (McKinsey) 71
Casey, Liam 193
Census Bureau 56
CES (Consumer Electronics
    Show) 8–9, 18–19
Chambers, John 14
Chauhan, Neeraj 66, 98
Chen, John 98, 127
Chesky, Bryan 85, 140
Chevy Volt (General Motors) 172
"Chief Listener & CEO" 122
China 27, 61, 62, 64–66, 69–72, 92,
    168, 193
Chino Farms 109
Chipotle 111
Christensen, Clayton 30, 45–46,
    153, 183
Churchill Club 188
Cisco 14
Clark, Jim 11, 33, 86
cloud and cloud computing ix,
    x, xi, 13–14, 16, 18, 20, 32, 38,
    40–41, 58, 76, 89, 90, 93–94,
    95, 97, 136, 144, 148, 150, 171,
    181–82, 191

Cloud Era 136
CMS (U.S. Medicare and Medicaid
  agency) 133
CNN 88
Coca-Cola and Coke 77–78, 112–13
Collins, Jim 138
Columbia University 174
Connect Smarter 66–68, 98
connect(ing) the dots 10, 90,
  147–48, 152, 172, 184
conspicuous consumption xv,
  55–57, 61, 64
consumer and consumer behav-
  ior ix, x, xi, xii, xiv, 11–12, 14, 15,
  16, 18, 19, 20, 21, 22, 23, 28–29,
  36, 41, 43, 48, 51–72, 75, 77–82,
  88, 97, 104, 106, 110–16, 132, 133,
  134–35, 136, 143, 148, 151, 153,
  159, 161, 176, 182, 188, 192, 193
Consumer Electronics Show
  (CES) 8–9, 18–19
Consumer Reports 111
Control Data 141
Cortana (Microsoft) xi, 19, 191
Cortlandt Street (NYC) 83
Costco 114
Crash of 2008 55–57
crowdfunding 39
Cupertino 3, 146
*Curious Case of Benjamin Button,
  The* 36
customer experience ix, x, xii,
  xiv, xv–xvi, 27, 28–29, 47, 69,
  76, 85, 88, 91, 93–95, 97, 99,
  100–16, 138, 149, 151, 161, 182,
  186, 188, 189, 193
customer metrics (satisfaction,
  acquisition cost, retention,
  lifetime value) xii, xiii, 28, 94,
  98, 104, 110, 112–16, 177, 188
customer–lifetime value xii, 28,
  102, 115
customer plan xii, xiii, 104, 151,
  153, 188
customer service 40, 102–3, 110,
  114
customer(s)-in-control ix–xiii,
  20–22, 23, 26, 108, 181, 216

Darwin, Charles 188
data modeling 15

data science xi, 15–18, 26, 94, 150,
  182
DEC PDP-11 135
deep dive(s) 136–7, 174, 184
Delhi (India) 98
Dell, Michael and Dell Inc. 86–87
Delta Airlines (LaGuardia
  Airport) 103–4
Diamandis, Peter 12–13
Diesel jeans xiv
Disney, The Walt (Company) 11
disruptive innovator and disruptive innovation 6, 7, 9, 153, 183
disruptive pricing xiv, xvi, 20, 21,
  28, 40, 41, 57, 64, 67–69, 76, 85,
  87–89, 91, 92–99, 103, 104, 106,
  107, 111, 149, 150, 153, 159, 160,
  181, 183, 186, 187
domain expertise xiii, 7–8, 11, 12,
  14, 18, 24, 25, 26, 27, 30, 36, 43,
  58, 67, 75, 82, 89–91, 98, 104,
  123, 128, 129–37, 140–41, 145,
  146, 148, 152, 153, 156, 158, 170–
  71, 177, 184, 186, 187, 195
Donald Deskey Associates 79
DRAM memory 9
driverless cars 6
Drucker, Peter F. 75, 144, 155, 189
Duffield, David 89
Duffy, John 176
DuPont 78
Dynabook 135

E2E (Emerging-to-Emerging
  Country trade) 61
Eagle, The 5
Eastern Europe 63, 70
eBay 20, 65
e-books 41
e-commerce 19, 24, 76
Economist, The 58, 123
Edison, Thomas 7, 119, 121, 188
EDS 87
800razors.com 97
Einstein, Albert 32, 38, 83
Eisenhower, President Dwight
  and administration 53
eLance 194
Ellison, Larry 9, 89
emergency room (health care)
  42–43, 81

emerging economies 61–72
emerging markets xiv, 61–72, 98,
190
emerging middle class 61–72
end-to-end (system) x, 10–12, 20,
21, 30, 34, 35, 79, 82, 90, 96, 105,
133, 148, 153, 189, 191, 193
entrepreneur and entrepreneurship x, xii–xiii, xv, 3, 9, 21, 22,
23, 24, 26, 32, 33, 36, 38, 42, 44,
45, 63, 64, 86, 87, 88, 91, 99,
105, 106, 107, 109, 119, 121, 129,
130, 132, 139, 141, 142, 143, 148,
154–69, 170–77, 181–83, 186,
190, 193, 194
Ethernet 22
Etsy 195
Eventbrite 77, 100
Exabyte 13

Facebook 21–23, 41, 64, 75, 177
failure xii, 11, 42, 80, 121, 122, 127, 134,
155–69, 172, 176, 184, 188, 195
Fairfield University 44–45
Fast Company 143
fast-food restaurant chains 54,
110–11
Father Knows Best 54
Feastly 195
feature creep 147–48
feature phone 18, 68
Federal-Aid Highway Act 53
Financial Stability Board 39
Financial Times 39, 123
Fire Phone (Amazon) 28–29
Firefly technology (Amazon) 29
Fitzgerald, Fr. Paul 44–45
Fletcher School Council for
Emerging Market Enterprises
(Tufts University) 63
floppy disk and floppy disk drive
8–9
Forbes 39, 144, 162
Ford Motor 141
Four Seasons Hotels and Resorts
101
Foxconn 98
Free Agent Nation (Daniel Pink)
143, 195
free-agent economy and nation
59, 143–44, 194–95

Friedman, Thomas 69–70, 141
"Frugal Fashionista" 72
Fusion-io 90
Future Agency 191

Gallup 56
Gannon, Tim 110–11
Gansky, Lisa 194
Gardner, Howard 135
Gassée, Jean-Louis 164, 185
Gates, Bill 9, 10, 23–24, 33–35, 108,
140
Gates, Melinda 35
GE (General Electric) 14, 46, 52
Gebbia, Joe 85, 140
General Electric 14, 46, 52
General Motors (GM) 71, 172
Genius Bar (Apple) 105
genomics 32
Germany 168
GI Bill 53
Gilboa, David 96
Gittleman, Dan 157–58
Gladwell, Malcolm 129
GM (General Motors) 71, 172
Good Earth restaurant, The 146
Good to Great (Jim Collins) 138
Google xi, 6, 12, 14–15, 19, 20, 28, 30,
101, 106, 111, 114, 122, 126, 141,
149–50, 165, 172, 174
Google Labs 6, 15
GPS 12, 15
graphene 13
Great Recession 39–40, 55–56
Grove, Andy 23, 44
Guangzhou (China) 62
Gujarat (India) 66
Gutenberg, Johannes 4

H.J. Heinz 80
hagwon 63
Hair Cuttery 107
Hakone (Japan) 18
Hangzhou (China) 65
Hartz, Julia 77, 100
Hartz, Kevin 100
Harvard Business School 30,
45–46
Harvard School of Education 135
Harvard University 43, 45
Hauser, Hermann 165

NOTES

1   In an insightful article in *Wired* in 2013, Astro Teller's perceptive in-
    sights include: "It's often *easier* to make something 10 times better
    than it is to make it 10 percent better. Yes . . . really. Because when
    you're working to make things 10 percent better, you inevitably fo-
    cus on the existing tools and assumptions. . . . [W]hen you aim for a
    10✗ gain, you lean instead on bravery and creativity—the kind that,
    literally and metaphorically, can put a man on the moon. . . . [B]ig-
    ger challenges create passion. And that, counter-intuitively, makes
    the hardest things much easier to accomplish than you might think."
    "Google ✗ Head on Moonshots: 10✗ Is Easier Than 10 Percent."
    Wired, Feb. 11, 2013: http://www.wired.com/2013/02/moonshots-
    matter-heres-how-to-make-them-happen/.

2   I make this point again, but it cannot be stressed too much: While
    exponentially advancing technologies are enabling the customer-
    in-control Moonshot to happen, the new businesses that result
    are often not technological in nature. They can be in the domains
    of rather routine products and services, designed by creative en-
    trepreneurs who are **not** technical engineers but who are offering
    customers options in new and often disruptively priced ways.
    "The Customer is Now in Control - Get Over It!" *Forbes*, May 2,
    2011:   http://www.forbes.com/sites/jimblasingame/2011/05/02/
    customer-in-control/.
    "Customer in control: The future of shopping is already here and
    retailers are battling to keep up." *Financial Review*, Nov. 7, 2013:
    http://www.afr.com/p/tech-gadgets/customer_battling_control_
    keep_future_LpY5jpjs859eMDlpF5vZ3K/.